Clifford Harrison

Stray records

Personal and professional notes

Clifford Harrison
Stray records
Personal and professional notes
ISBN/EAN: 9783337276836

Printed in Europe, USA, Canada, Australia, Japan

Cover: Foto ©Andreas Hilbeck / pixelio.de

More available books at **www.hansebooks.com**

STRAY RECORDS

OR

PERSONAL AND PROFESSIONAL NOTES

BY

CLIFFORD HARRISON

IN TWO VOLUMES

VOL. I

LONDON
RICHARD BENTLEY AND SON
Publishers in Ordinary to Her Majesty the Queen
1892

(All rights reserved)

TO

WILLIAM HARRISON,

AND

HERBERT HARDINGE,—

MY FRIEND-BROTHER, AND MY BROTHER-FRIEND,—

I DEDICATE THIS BOOK.

PREFATORY NOTE.

I HAVE selected and arranged these notes during the days of my sojourn at Montreux, recovering, as I hope, from a long illness. The note-books from which they are taken are before me as I write, thirty in number. The first has for its opening date October 25, 1879, and the last entry in volume thirty is January 7, 1889.

The time-honoured prefatory statement on the part of an author—that he had no thought of publication 'when he wrote the following pages'—is really too old and decrepit a friend to make his appearance nowadays without some sort of apology. Yet he meets me with insistent demands for a place on the very threshold of this volume. So I must make the best of him, and ask indulgence for his grey hairs, because in this instance they are honourable. He takes his stand on this page, for it is his by right; and his words, though so well known, are true. But although when I wrote my note-books it was absolutely without an 'afterthought' of publication, yet I will own that the idea that I should some day 'do something with them' was, as they advanced in number, constantly presented to me by her for whom they were written—my mother. Indeed the knowledge that it was her earnest wish that the note-books should be gathered sooner or later into printed form is my first and strongest reason for publishing this volume.

When I began to write these note-books I was very busy. Nearly every day I had a recital somewhere, in town or country. The country engagements involved a great deal of travelling. My memory for the little events and episodes of daily life is treacherous, and my power of narrating them a most uncertain quantity. But everything that happened to me had its interest for my mother, who lived with me. Urged thereto by a friend, I therefore began to jot down, day by day, anything and everything that I thought would amuse her to read of. The reward was great; for her interest in the little volumes grew with them. I recollect now, with more unmixed pleasure than is found in the texture of most memories, that she generally had one of these same volumes by her side or in her workbasket. In its pages I talked to her, and told her all I did, and still more all I thought. In that last word lies—as I feel it—one of the many weaknesses of this present volume. Yet it is one that must exist in the very nature of its origin. For she would often, in 'mock heroics,' quote Elena's words from *Philip van Artevelde*, and say—

'The loud transactions of the outlying world
  Tell to your masculine friends : tell me your thoughts.'

And so I used to write of what I thought quite as much as of what I did; and whether it was 'occurrences of thought' or of event, I wrote it all in the way I hoped would best please her. Such, however, would not be the way I should have written,, nor should I have selected the same matter from my life to narrate, had I been conscious that it would one day take unto itself the dignity of print, and run the responsibility of publication.

But my hope is that the very homeliness of the form may make the notes acceptable to some readers, although it may deter others. And certain it is that, for good or ill, the pages must go forth as they were written, and that if any spirit is to be preserved in them, it cannot be other than that which actuated my pen whilst—often hurriedly and at the end of hard-working days, but always in the knowledge of the sympathy that would read the words—I wrote the notes from which I have built up this old-fashioned sort of book.

Old-fashioned. I use the expression with

meaning; for that, as I believe—and I will add, as I hope—is the note struck in these pages. In our days of the *fin du siècle*, when the thought of the hour has grown so definite that it has coined a word and called itself Modernity, it is very hazardous, clearly, for an unimportant person to dare to say his work is old-fashioned. Is it not self-condemnation? To many, doubtless, it is. To others I hope it may even put forth a claim to liking and favour. At least of that I must take the chance. But I give the word with an unfaltering hand, and leave it to sound, according to the ear that listens, its note of warning or of invitation.

In selecting pages from my note-books, I found that many of the least dull passages had to be rejected. In such work it is difficult to know where to draw the line of silence. To judge by the signs of the times it would seem to be better to be indiscreet than dull: dullness is the worst form of indiscretion. Still, as I have to plead guilty to that form of the vice, let me not add to it the further indiscretion of seeming forgetful of certain laws of hospitality after I have been so generously accorded its privileges. Thus many pages have had to be put aside, some of them bearing names which could give an interest to any page, others recording kindness and friendship which, at least to me, need no page to keep their remembrance bright; and yet again others, which would be the very pages to be read by many people with the greatest zest, as possessing that peculiar quality of interest whose charm is that the reader is therein conscious of an edge.

Yet, although I have rejected much, I have the fear that I may have still been guilty of keeping too much. I hope I may be pardoned in this, if I have preserved to a fault the attitude of a private note-book. I should be sorry to give offence to any. I have endeavoured, wherever I could, and wherever it was possible, to weave the disjointed notes together; but often, and perhaps at best, the pages are sadly fragmentary.

Let me deprecate, too, any severe criticism of such opinions as I have ventured on in these records. Such passages are not put forward in any way as professional criticisms, but merely as the opinions of one who loves what is artistic and beautiful; and having been born in this generation cannot help being critical even in his likings and admirations. We are nothing if not critical in these days. Criticism of some kind or another, therefore, may be said to be an instinct of self-preservation. As such only let it stand in this volume.

Three years is a long time in these busy days—a perilously long time—for a public artist to be away from his post. Small wonder if he be forgotten and his place should know him no more. It is an honest, as it is a pleasant, surprise to me when I find any sign that I and my work are in any sort of way still remembered. I have had to accept, with such patience as I could muster, the stern if benignant lessons of a very long illness. I loved my work, and it seemed as if I had just touched assurance in it, when I was silenced. A deep sorrow, which is still a present one, has also visited me. This place has worked out for me this season of denial and loss.

Sitting here in my little salon and watching a glorious sunset—where the long blue line of the far-off Jura alone divides the splendour of the sky from the answering splendour of the lake—I write these last lines for this volume. This room has many memories for me: not the least of them will be those which gather round these pages.

HOTEL BREUER, MONTREUX,
    1891.

I.
NOTES OF MY WORK.

> '*Polonius.* What do you read, my lord?
> *Hamlet.* Words, words, words!'
> *Shakespeare.*

STRAY RECORDS.

I.

Of what nature is it?—My first recital—Criticism—Recitations with music—Beethoven's *Egmont*—The aim of recitation—Choice of recitations—Repertory of recitations—' Following' the reciter—Applause—Recitals at private parties—Some criticisms—Candour—A curious experience—Another kind of experience—Sense of humour—' Only for fun'—Humour illustrated—A curious supper party—A letter—' D.V.'—A form of Catechism—A phantom recital—Recital at Christchurch, Oxford—Personal interest—A novel entertainment—' Nothing to see'—The appeal to the ear—An evening of defeat—A tribute—Recital at the Prince's Hall—Recital at Sandringham—Difficulty of choosing pieces for private recitals—Recitation.

I WAS talking to a man at Montreux in the December of 1890, and, perhaps somewhat foolishly, permitted myself in the course of conversation to speak of 'my work,' and of my hope that I might shortly be well enough to resume that work. 'May I ask the nature of the work to which you refer?' he said pleasantly. 'Presumably it is the Bar, since you speak of the necessity of recovering your voice. Pardon me for inquiring.'

Once again. When I first began my long sojourn of convalescence in Switzerland, I met a lady who was devoted to reciting. She herself was a 'star' in the amateur firmament. She narrated to me her triumphs, and told me that nothing in the world excited and pleased her so much as reciting, or, as she unselfishly added, hearing somebody else recite. She ended up by saying, 'Perhaps you, like so many men, don't care about reciting. But did you—did you ever try it yourself?'

These two wholesome experiences point out to me that the heading of this section—'Notes of my Work'—had best be explained, lest a worse thing befall me.

I started very early in life as an actor. I was not eighteen when I left home for my first engagement at the Theatre Royal, Manchester. In less than a year I quitted the stage, and went to college with the intention of entering the Church. This plan, however, was soon given up, and with its resignation I left Cambridge. I then took up painting. But I could not afford definite technical training. I worked very hard, but it was in my own room and after my own method. Such work in art is often labour wasted. If not wholly wasted in my case, it proved no road to the necessary professional skill which, unassisted by other elements, alone holds its own in the world, and (terrible but necessary test!) 'makes a living' for the artist. I went on the stage again, of course. My last regular engagement on the stage was at the St. James's Theatre, under the management of Mrs. John Wood—an introduction that has since developed into a most kind and pleasant friendship. When that engagement ended, it was necessary to do something more definite toward the accomplishment of that curious practical problem—making both ends meet—than I could find with my brush and easel.

I determined to give a 'Reading.' At the moment little more was planned by it than that it should tide over the time being. I took St. George's Hall for the occasion. Friends aided me, and I spoke a few pieces at afternoon parties. The success I received began to make me hopeful. I put a footnote in the programme of my recital to say I would accept engagements, public and private. That was on the 14th of February, 1877. Before the end of the season I had almost more work than I could accept.

Since that time I have been increasingly busy. I have given myself a two-months' holiday each year, in the late summer. But all the rest of the year I have worked hard in London and in the provinces. Often in the London season I have had two engagements a day. The average all the year round, including the holiday time—until 1888, when I was taken ill in the November—was five recitals a week. Thus, in those eleven years and nine months, I gave over three thousand performances.

It is a sharp and increasing regret to me that for so many years I was unable to appeal systematically to public audiences. I was often strongly urged to risk a long series of public recitals, but my means did not, to my mind, justify the risk and responsibility. For I can honestly say I mistrusted myself, and did not consider that the scheme would answer, or gain success. I was nearly six years hard at work every day, in private, or for charities, or for occasions organized by those who were less doubtful of the result than I was. Then at last I tried a series of four public recitals in London. The next year I gave eleven; then twelve, which were so successful that I immediately added another series of twelve, thus making the longest series on record—lasting from January to July. For the next two years I gave this series of twenty-four recitals, every Saturday afternoon, at the Steinway Hall. The rest of the weeks I took for country and private engagements. But illness stopped my work in 1888; and since then I have only been able to give a few short series when health has been granted to me.

The most fatiguing part of my work lay in the constant travelling. I am a poor traveller, and when I began to accept country engagements I felt the journeys very much. But the parallel of the eel holds more or less good in most cases of custom; and at last I managed pretty well in my journeyings hither and thither. I got to know the peculiarities of the various lines—which jolts, and which runs easily, which is punctual and which steals time in the proverbial manner. The officials on many of the lines entered into my list of acquaintances, and I developed a practical knowledge of the geography of England, which would have been invaluable in my school examinations. By my note-books I find that some weeks were peculiarly marked by erratic wanderings. For example, I find London, Edinburgh, London, Bournemouth, Birmingham, Tring, and London again, are recorded in one of my note-books as the headings of one week's work; and another week gives me Bolton, Bristol, Exeter, Dover, Liverpool, and London, as the places visited. These were, doubtless, exceptionally hard weeks as far as travelling went; but, although the distances traversed were above the average, the amount of work represented was by no means exceptional. In a regularly organized tour of public performances no such rushing about is necessary, as places are taken in order and fit in with one another. But in my work, as far as it was possible, I accepted the engagements that offered, irrespective of the journeys they involved, save in the mere question of the Time Tables. Yet, the recitals being often private, or merely locally announced, I have been greeted in London by a professional friend—whose work, though much more advertised, was, I was quite sure, much less arduous than mine,—with, 'Well, and where have you been hiding all this time? You take it pretty easy after the season is over!'

Not the least amusing part of my work lay in the fact that it was singularly varied in the audience it appealed to, and in the grades of society through which it passed. In one day I have, as it were, struck one of the lowest and one of the highest notes on the gamut of what is called Society. I have had experiences of all sorts and conditions of drawing-rooms. Few professional artists would have such opportunities. Singers, for instance, do not often find themselves on the lower rungs of the social ladder in their work. A concert is a costly thing. But a reciter who gives the whole entertainment is more or less within reach of all who give parties. It is certain that he has a wide area of experience in this matter. Let me be pardoned for taking the work of another week, which will exemplify this fact.

Monday.—Recital at an 'At Home,' Eaton Place.

Tuesday.—Evening recital at Mechanics' Institute, near Birmingham.

Wednesday.—Recital at Park House, Sandringham (Lady Probyn's). The Princess of Wales present; Prince Albert Victor and the Princesses Louise, Victoria, and Maude of Wales, etc.

Thursday.—Evening recital at a boys' school at St. Leonards.

Friday.—Evening recital at a suburban party at Sydenham.

Saturday.—My own public recital at the Steinway Hall, in the afternoon. In the evening, recite at an 'At Home" in Belgrave Square.

The question might naturally arise hence,—Which audience did I find the best?—or, possibly, the still more interesting one—Which did I find the worst? But ah! who is expected to reveal his state secrets? Only let me say that, as a rule, I like all my audiences, save those of the typical smart London drawing-room. To be perfectly truthful, then,—for once,—I have no hesitation in saying that, taking the week I have quoted, the best audiences were those of the Wednesday evening and of the Saturday afternoon.

I should be ungrateful to an important factor in the public life of every artist, if I were not to speak of the wonderful and generous support I have received from the public press. Newspaper criticism of art has been discussed and called in question so much of late, that it is a pleasant duty for an artist to be able to say that he has nearly always found it kindly; and that to him, whether kindly or unfavourable, it has always been perfectly spontaneous. All my life I have seen and heard too much of theatrical and 'professional' life not to know the enormous practical influence and value of 'notices' to any one whose work is on the boards or the platform. The artistic use and value of criticism will, no doubt, always be, under present conditions, a point for argument and difference of opinion. But of its practical power over the fortunes of an artist there can be no question. It has not been in the way, either of my life or of my inclination, to court the favour of those who wield this power; and my conviction is that any such courting would be, in most cases, a very fruitless quest. I am glad to know that through my work I have made the acquaintance and friendship of some of the gentlemen who are well-known in the world of public criticism. I value highly the words—printed, written, and spoken—I have recived from them. I think it is pardonable to be proud of such words as these—taken from a letter to me from Mr. Clement Scott,—and I hope I may be pardoned for quoting them—

'You can convey a poet to the sense of an audience as no man has ever done it before in my memory for twenty-five years. You have done more for poetry than any man of your time. . . . Last season, the happiest and most intellectual hours I spent were under your extraordinary power and sympathy. You make me take down my books and read. When you have put a poem in our hearts, you persuade us to give it to others. . . .'

To preserve a sense of proportion is always healthy. Thus I recollect once when I was in the midst of my six months' series of recitals at the Steinway Hall, when we turned money away every Saturday, and the London press had given me the fullest measure of encouragement and praise, I went to some provincial city—Norwich, I think it certainly was—to recite at a concert, and thereon received, in the columns of one of the local papers, the following notice: 'Mr. Harrison, if he felt so disposed, might, we are really inclined to believe, almost undertake an entertainment by himself, to which possibly many persons might be happy to go.' I came to town a wiser and a sadder man.

There is no greater pleasure to me than arranging one of my musical recitations.

Practically the work is full of interest. To begin with, it is difficult to say why certain pieces suggest musical accompaniment. Some poems, which gain most by music, have no actual hint of it in them. Occasionally, of course, on the other hand, the hint is clear, as in Browning's *Saul*, Tennyson's *Amphion*, and Longfellow's *Monk Felix*. Yet it is certain that the 'cue' for music must not be too obvious, nor the suggestion of the sound too clearly stated, or a commonplaceness, a realistic element, altogether unpoetic, not to say vulgar, will be introduced. Even when the suggestion is answered and carried out, it must be very carefully done—suggestive more than expressive. Such a poem as Edgar Allen Poe's *The Bells* is almost too suggestive. There is grave danger of vulgarity and absurdity in a musical accompaniment. Anything like an attempt at imitation would be fatal. When I arranged my recitation of it (I did not attempt it until long after I had given the *Raven*, which I think far more suited to musical accompaniment, though of 'music' it has no hint), I carefully avoided all attempt to imitate bells, taking the tone and emotion of each passage rather than the fact it describes.

Known tunes are, as a rule, to be avoided. I always had this instinct, and experience soon proved to me that it was a true one. The reason is clear. A melody that is well known is associated in the mind of the listener with certain thoughts — perhaps personal memories—and even, if it be a song-tune, with positive words. Directly the tune is heard these associations are stirred into assertion, and in few cases will the assertion be anything else but disturbing and detrimental to the direct line of the imagination required. In one case only have I found well-known tunes effective. In Dickens's *Christmas Carol* I introduce *Hark ! the herald angels sing*, and *Home, sweet Home*. The associations started are clear and universal, and, for once, they work in true parallel with the emotions of the passages recited. People turn and look at each other and smile a kindly smile—the sort of smile that suits the story—when they hear the old tunes. But that is the only case I know where such an effect is wholly desirable. That turning and smiling, which is certain to follow the introduction of a well-known tune, is fatal, as a rule. It is just the sort of movement, physical and mental, one wishes to guard against in an audience. In Tennyson's *Ode on the Death of the Duke of Wellington* it was impossible to refuse to introduce the 'Dead March' from *Saul*—' Hush, the Dead March wails in the people's ears;' and the effect in a way is good. Only, alas! that rustle of recognition is nearly sure to follow, to the detriment of the sustained emotion. It just ruffles the even surface and flow of the feeling wrought by the verse. In Lord Lytton's *At the Opera*, to introduce *Ah! che la morte* would simply ruin and vulgarize the whole beauty of the poem. Every one knows the tune. Some may love it; many, we know, loathe it. In the recitation one wants neither the one feeling nor the other. Perhaps conscious of this himself, the author has, wisely I think, in the later edition of the poem, cut out the verses that certify the occasion and the actual song and singer. What one wants at such a time in an audience is a perfectly disengaged attention and a highly emotionalized imagination. Music can give good aid to both these attitudes of feeling, but it must be music without ready-made associations.

In nearly all cases I have myself composed the musical accompaniment I use. I always begin by searching for something that will work in, but it is strange how rarely I find anything that wholly suits. Whenever I do, I accept it with delight, and feel the recitation will gain thereby. In the *High Tide on the Coast of Lincolnshire* I play an old English air—*The Legend of the Avon.* In Alfred Austin's *In the Month when sings the Cuckoo* I employ, as a 'motive,' worked out into many forms, a part-song of Macfarren's in *She stoops to conquer.* In Eric Mackay's *Beethoven at the Piano* I play the first movement of the *Moonlight* sonata. In George Macdonald's *Legend of Sir Aglovaile* I recite the song to Sterndale Bennett's *Forget-me-not.* These, with a few bars from *Faust* in *King Robert of Sicily*, and the instances I named in the *Christmas Carol* and the *Ode to Wellington,* are, I think, the only occasions on which I have employed music not my own.

Great accuracy is needed in these accompanied recitations. The rhythm of the music and the verse may often seem distinct, but in reality they must be in sympathy. They work, indeed, separately, and on different levels; but at points—in certain lines—often in a word, a syllable—they must meet with unfailing certainty. The correspondence must never for a moment drop, although it must always be carried on out of sight.

One of the chief difficulties a reciter accompanying himself has to conquer is, that he must look as little as possible at the keyboard of the piano. It seems a small point, but it is a most necessary one. First, because the music must, as far as possible, be an ideal thing, apart from the idea of any special instrument, and to look at the keyboard emphasizes the fact of the piano. Second, because a reciter must always keep his eyes for the service of facial expression. The hands must therefore do their own work in the accompaniment; and even of them he may sometimes have to claim other service; in which case the music must be discontinued, or the left hand must sustain it alone. It is necessary therefore to practise the music, until it is known so well, and the distances are measured so truly, that it can be performed without the player looking at his hands.

The recitation must, in fact, always be pre-eminent.

I once read—recited—spoke—(I don't know what word to use)—the text to Beethoven's *Egmont.* It was at St. James's Hall (Friday, May 12, 1882). The task is always a difficult one, and on this occasion the result—from my point of view—was lamentable, although it was pronounced to possess the usual measure of success. Let me hasten to add that there was, therefore, nothing lamentable in the performance of the music. That had received all due care. The orchestra was a splendid one, and Sir Charles Hallé conducted. It was the idea and scheme of the whole work, taken in its full stature and proportion, which seemed to me so misrepresented. For I take it that the idea —the scheme—is one of drama—drama, illustrated by music and declamation woven together into one poetic appeal.

It was peculiarly interesting to me, as it ought to be a masterful and perfect expression of the art I attempt in my own recitations with music.

As the subject enters very truly into these notes on my work, I venture to quote a paragraph or two from an article I wrote on Recitation. The paragraphs were originally taken from one of my note-books, and therefore I feel it is permissible to quote them here.

Giving, as I often do, months of careful thought and constant practice to the preparation of even some short poem set to my own accompaniment of music, I cannot forget my feelings when, late on the last rehearsal, on the very day of the concert, I was asked to go up on the platform and 'run through the words with the band.' I was placed close to the eminent conductor, directly beneath his arm, as it were, he standing over me at his desk. The position assigned to me, I saw at once, rendered action of any kind as impossible as it would have been ridiculous. I was hemmed in by violinists whose bow-arms nearly touched me at every stroke. Several of the gentlemen very kindly and courteously tried to move back, to their own inconvenience, so as to give me more room. At each cue for the band there was the audible tap of the *bâton*. We tried it over once. What dramatic effect was possible? Yet dramatic effect, I contend, should be the real note of the performance; not, indeed, the dramatic effect of the footlights and the stage, but of declamation and music joined in one great appeal. I believe Beethoven would have been the first to own this. One hears in all the music the voice of the dramatic instinct. Such a performance might be most impressive. But it would require most careful arrangement and thought, many and accurate rehearsals, and the co-operation of every one concerned.

I am willing to own that I do not yet see how recitation with music can be made effective under the conditions which usually mark the combination. At present the only chance of success seems to be for one and the same person to give both words and music. He is then master of the means employed. And it appears necessary that he should be master, and that the means employed should be under his control—or rather under the control of the drama he enunciates. With great practice and an unusually swift understanding and sympathy, a coherent work might be made between a reciter and an accompanist, or even between a reciter and a band. But the latter would require the devotion and labour given to an opera at Bayreuth, instead of the casual and slipshod combination that is too often attempted on such occasions.*

There can be no question of the power of appeal to many people in this combination of poetry with music. Musicians have felt it, but have attacked it, until lately, I venture to think, from the wrong side. Actors and reciters have felt it, but they have lacked the mastery of the accompanying art. Mr. Bellew, years ago, used to give certain pieces with organ accompaniment, and with an unseen chorus.

When I began my work I did not attempt the combination. It was a long time before I in any way satisfied myself over it. It was, in effect, a new thing when I first gave accompanied recitations. I suppose I must count imitation as the sincere flattery we are told of. But I could have been content with less of it!

* Let me add that I am told that, during my long sojourn out of England, much has been done toward the perfecting a performance of this kind. I have read and heard much of Dr. A. C. Mackenzie's *Dream of Jubal*, and the declamation of Miss Julia Neilson in the descriptive text. One may reasonably hope that so fine a combination as that of music and poetry will be developed and perfected in time into a noble form of dramatic expression.

For after about a year or so I found that recitations with music were common features at entertainments, though I think they have been always given by an accompanist with the reciter.

I will candidly own to being proud of having made this new style of recitation popular.

Mr. Henry Irving tried the effect in that grisly story *The Uncle*, music for which was composed by Sir Julius Benedict. Mr. Corder has composed music for a translation of Uhland's *The Minstrel's Curse*. Dr. Mackenzie has given us the cantata of *The Dream of Jubal*. I was gratified to receive a letter from Mr. Corder, in which he says: 'Yesterday I had for the first time the opportunity of hearing you recite' (Brighton, Nov., 1887). 'Speaking as a musician, I must say that I never before realized how enormously the passion and pathos of poetry could be intensified by the aid of music really artistically applied.' The encouragement I have received from musical friends has pleased me greatly, as being a sign that the combination appeals to them in its wonderful suggestiveness. It is, of course, unpopular with certain listeners of the technically literary attitude of mind, and with those to whom music is only a sound, and not an endlessly intelligent and suggestive voice. But the vote of the majority is distinctly in favour and strong approval of the combination.

Schumann and Liszt arranged several ballads for recitation with music. Musically these works are fine, but I have been told that they have never gained their due effect. I do not believe they ever will. For, fine as they are, splendid as the music is—as music,—they have the radical fault of misconception. They are pre-eminently musical; they should be pre-eminently declamatory. Mendelssohn's *Athalie* has held its own best, because in it the necessary conditions are the best observed.

But if musicians had understood and accepted the relative positions of the two appeals in this combination, what a splendid result might have been attained! Wagner would surely have given the world a work of this sort that would have marked a new departure in art, for he was before all things a Sound-Poet. I always like to believe that had this form of dramatic expression been presented to him in all its fine possibilities, he would have grasped its suggestion to the full, and given us a grand and perfect example of this new recitative.

A thoroughly sympathetic audience is a perfect enjoyment to any public artist. If his listeners find any pleasure in the performance it is because they, with him, live for the time being in the work of the author represented.

That, I think, should be the aim of all reciting—to live, and make the hearers live, on the spoken words. If this be attained, and the poet's words are realized, then speaker and audience are for the moment raised to the poet's level.

But at first this can be hardly attained. Therefore it is that so many authors and people of the highest literary and imaginative faculty care but little, broadly speaking, for the stage and for dramatic declamation. They already feel and see in the printed page all, and more than all, that actor or reciter can represent or even hint at. To them the acted drama, or the dramatically recited poem, is actually less dramatic than their own realization of the play or the verse. The very means employed to quicken imagination and aid realization are to them so many detriments to the one and limits to the other. They do not, in fact, need any such means.

But for most people these means are useful in the highest degree. By their employment an approach is made to the poet's level and standpoint. The printed page to the ordinary reader means, in degree, much, little, or nothing. But at its best of 'much' it means less than good acting or reciting can give to it. The speaker or actor, therefore, employing the means of dramatic declamation, is thus to them, for the time being, the poet himself, and enables them to become, as it were, inhabitants of the poet's world. Yet the most skilful artist cannot give the life and illumination which filled the poet when he wrote his lines. The finest dramatic performance is probably as much under the level of the poet's conception and ideal, as it is above that of the usual reader.

Thus I am never surprised when I see or hear that an author or person of great literary capability cares little for my work. And, let me add with all respect, I never care to see such people present. Browning was the most unprejudiced, most open-minded listener I have known amongst poets, and the most perceptive of the art of dramatic expression. Mathew Arnold was the next. Mr. Ruskin listened—as it seemed to me—with an ear so attentive to the words and so already formed in judgment for or against certain authors that a disengaged imagination and criticism of the means of dramatic expression became of necessity secondary matters. A friend once offered to ask Miss Jean Ingelow to come and hear me recite *High Tide on the Coast of Lincolnshire*, but I found no courage to accept the offer. 'Ouida' wished to hear me give a passage I recite from her *Signa*, but the words fled from me at the idea. What reciting of *The Brook* or of *The Lotus-Eaters* could fulfil the Laureate's own realization of the lovely lines ? It seems to me clear, and on the face of things evident, that poets and authors (save, indeed, those who work in the department of letters practically connected with 'the drama' —but that exception scarcely needs statement) should not, in the very nature and character of their art, greatly care for vocal dramatic expression, especially that of recitation; its work, save in the matter of technical personal skill in the means employed, is included in their own.

CHOICE OF RECITATIONS.

One of the most difficult parts of my work—as it must be of any reciter's—is the choice of pieces for recitation. The work is all the more difficult because it must be almost entirely a matter of personal taste and judgment. Actors, singers, instrumentalists, have at least one half of their work in combination with other artists working to one complete performance. As a rule the responsibility of the choice of material rests with no one of them in particular. But a reciter is wholly and absolutely responsible alike for manner and matter. The great stock pieces for recitation have by this time become so hackneyed that they are almost useless, and the chief demand of an audience is for something new.

I have found the best novelty in old pages. I own to having a dread of the modern colloquial recitation, cast on the first person singular, and with an imaginary 'sir' who asks questions. I soon felt that recitation would be unable to hold its own as an art, and that no reciter could go on appealing to audiences week after week, unless his programmes had a certain literary value as well as dramatic interest.

There is a temptation to speak certain

poems or passages of prose because one loves them. But that is one of the worst reasons for choosing them. The test must be—do they gain by dramatic recitation? Many poems of great beauty, and even of great drama, do not gain by being spoken dramatically. They rather lose by the process. The chief beauty of the poem may be its form and music, and both may be somewhat jarred and disturbed by exhibitions of personal emotion and dramatic utterance; or the drama may be taken from the literary point of view, and its very excellencies, judged thence, may be mistakes from the declamatory point of view. Or the drama may be impossible for a public audience.

And, above all, a recitation, whether grave or humorous, must be submitted to a fiery ordeal of possible humour. Reciting is perilously girt about with opportunities for sinning against the Genius of humour; and he is a god whom it is dangerous to sin against, for his revenges are cruel and punctual. He is a great god and a powerful, a merry god and a kind—in his way. But he is withal absolutely indifferent and ruthless, and he knows well that he can never assert himself more triumphntly than when he is forgotten. He leaps around the class-room; he pops up in church; he has appeared at funerals; he is in the prompter's box at all tragedies; and he sits in the front row at every recital. His laughter rings out in derision with alarming promptitude. He has no pity. I know no place where he is more ready for mischief than on the platform of a reciter. Possibly the common-place but important fact that the speaker is clothed 'in his habit, as he lives,' is the basis at the outset of a ludicrous possibility of incongruity which may be seized on at any moment, or which only needs some unfortunate, imperceptible touch to be obvious to everybody. Whether this be so or not, it is certain that the Genius of humour places a peculiarly mischievous elf by the side of a reciter, who will seize on any, the slightest, vantage ground, and in a moment turn his work into defeat of a very inglorious kind. To keep this spirit dormant and powerless is one of the chief tasks of such an artist. I think it is almost as difficult to keep this spirit at bay when you don't want him, as it is to gain his co-operation when you do!

'Slips' of memory, as they are called, are very curious and seem to defy all rule or forethought. And yet it is certain that some authors lend themselves to this treachery of memory in a curious and unaccountable way. Some people have thought it strange that I should be able to remember long passages of Carlyle and Walt Whitman. But, as a matter of fact, these authors are very easy to remember. Their sentences are so marked, so individual, so suggestively dramatic, that, once learnt, they fix themselves indelibly on the mind. The smooth, graceful diction of Prescott and Byron is incomparably more difficult to remember. To me the three most difficult authors to remember are Lewis Morris, Sir Francis Hastings Doyle, and Adelaide Anne Procter. I always have to study Lewis Morris's *Marsyas* before I recite it. Once I recollect making many 'slips' in it, which were the more annoying to me as the poet was present. I had recited the poem 'letter perfect' the day before. With his usual courtesy and kindness Mr. Lewis Morris made light of the mistakes, and with his usual swift understanding he realized the position. And indeed I am sure he is too wide in his knowledge and love of the drama and its utterance to think verbal accuracy is its highest excellence. But it could not have disturbed any of my listeners more than it did me to hear the lines other than true to the text.

Many pieces I have learnt only to reject at once when thoroughly mastered, or but to make a trial of them. Some I have liked well enough for a time, but have soon grown weary of. At present the repertory I have accepted for myself and have at the command of memory and practice stands thus—

Lost and Found	.. *Hamilton Aïde.*
George Lee	.. *Hamilton Aïde.*
The Story of Two Lives	.. *Hamilton Aïde.*
The Song of the Engine	.. *James Anderson.*
Tristram and Iseult	.. *Matthew Arnold.*
The Forsaken Merman	.. *Matthew Arnold.*
The Buried Life	.. *Matthew Arnold.*
Poor Matthias	.. *Matthew Arnold.*
*At Bethlehem	.. *Edwin Arnold.*
*The Great Renunciation ..	.. *Edwin Arnold.*
A Rajpût Nurse	.. *Edwin Arnold.*
The Snake	.. *Edwin Arnold.*
*He and She	.. *Edwin Arnold.*
Belshazzar's Feast	.. *Edwin Arnold.*
Grandmother Teaching	.. *Alfred Austin.*
*Ave Maria	.. *Alfred Austin.*
*In the Month when Sings the Cuckoo ..	*Alfred Austin.*
*The Poet	.. *Alfred Austin.*
*' If you were here '	.. *Alfred Austin.*
*Is Life worth Living ?	.. *Alfred Austin.*

Edinburgh after Flodden	*Aytoun.*
The Execution of Montrose	*Aytoun.*
The Knight and the Lady	*Barham.*
The Young Grey Head	*Caroline Bowles.*
*Saul	*Browning.*
*The Boy and the Angel	*Browning.*
Hervé Riel	*Browning.*
Martin Relph	*Browning.*
The Italian in England	*Browning.*
Holy Cross Day	*Browning.*
Garden Fancies	*Browning.*
Up at a Villa	*Browning.*
A Toccata of Galuppi's	*Browning.*
Count Gismond	*Browning.*
The Pied Piper	*Browning.*
My Last Duchess	*Browning.*
How they brought Good News from Aix to Ghent	*Browning.*
Evelyn Hope	*Browning.*
The Naggletons on the Derby	*Shirley Brooks.*
*Mary Queen of Scots	*Bell.*
*The Isles of Greece	*Byron.*
*The Destruction of Sennacherib	*Byron.*
Waterloo	*Byron.*
The Ocean	*Byron.*
The Death of Manfred	*Byron.*
The Fall of Corinth	*Byron.*
The Dead Pan	*Mrs. Browning.*
*A Musical Instrument	*Mrs. Browning.*
The Rhyme of the Duchess May	*Mrs. Browning.*
Phil Blood's Leap	*Robert Buchanan.*
On Work	*Carlyle.*

REPERTORY.

The Night of Spurs	*Carlyle.*
Hero Worship	*Carlyle.*
On the Beach	*Calverley.*
Flight	*Calverley.*
A Ballad	*Calverley.*
Gemini and Virgo	*Calverley.*
The Last Man	*Campbell.*
Our Eye-witness on the Ice	*E. Collins.*
Conversation	*Cowper.*
*Stanzas	*Cowper.*
The Patronized Boy	*Crabbe.*
*A Christmas Carol (entire)	*Dickens.*
*An Adaptation of the *Chimes*	*Dickens.*
*The Dream of a Star	*Dickens.*
Mr. Harold Skimpole	*Dickens.*
Mr. Chadband's Oratory	*Dickens.*
Mr. Silas Wegg	*Dickens.*
Mr. and Mrs. Micawber	*Dickens.*
Sentiment	*Dickens.*
Mrs. Joseph Porter	*Dickens.*
The Parlour Orator	*Dickens.*
The Spanish Mother	*Doyle.*
The Doncaster St. Leger	*Doyle.*
The Red Thread of Honour	*Doyle.*
The Caliph and the Carpenter	*Austin Dobson.*
A Gentleman of the Old School	*Austin Dobson.*
To Lydia	*Austin Dobson.*
Incognita	*Austin Dobson.*
*Song on St. Cecilia's Day	*Dryden*
An Arresting Voice	*George Eliot.*
Mrs. Poyser 'has her say out'	*George Eliot.*
Mr. Gilfil	*George Eliot.*

Aunt Pullet's Bonnet	*George Eliot.*
Silas Marner's Comforters	*George Eliot.*
Armgart	*George Eliot.*
Scene from the *Spanish Gipsy*	*George Eliot.*
*A Prayer for Rest	*Ebenezer Elliott.*
Random Meditations (*The Bow of Ulysses*)	*Froude.*
Jupiter and Io	*Fields.*
The Owl Critic	*Fields.*
The Village Preacher	*Goldsmith.*
*The Building of St. Sophia	*Baring Gould.*
*Bishop Benno	*Baring Gould.*
*The Little Scholar	*Baring Gould.*
The Romance of Britomarte	*Lindsay Gordon.*
*The Bells of Ys	*Clifford Harrison.*
*The Statue	*Clifford Harrison.*
*The Silver Bell	*Clifford Harrison.*
A Son of Orpheus	*Clifford Harrison.*
Faithful unto Death	*Clifford Harrison.*
*A Farewell	*Clifford Harrison.*
The Signalman	*Clifford Harrison.*
Carcassonne	*Clifford Harrison.*
The Lost Galleon	*Bret Harte.*
How Santa Claus came to Simpson's Bar	*Bret Harte.*
Dow's Flat	*Bret Harte.*
*A Newport Romance	*Bret Harte.*
Jim Bludso	*John Hay.*
The House of Stradivarius	*Haweis.*
The Event of the Season	*Oliver Wendell Holmes.*
The Return of the Witches	*Oliver Wendell Holmes.*
A Practical Joke	*Theodore Hook.*
Chacun à son goût	*Theodore Hook.*
Domestic Asides	*Hood.*

An Incendiary Song	Hood.
Our Village	Hood.
The Dream of Eugene Aram	Hood.
The Poor	Victor Hugo.
*High Tide on the Coast of Lincolnshire	Jean Ingelow.
Stage Land	J. K. Jerome.
A Gossip on Cats and Dogs	J. K. Jerome.
A Reminiscence of Charles Kingsley, including—	
The Air Mothers	Kingsley.
Ode to the North-East Wind	Kingsley.
The Ballad of Lorraine	Kingsley.
The Story of the Mayor of Plymouth	Kingsley.
The Sea Fight, from *Westward Ho!*	Kingsley.
*On Music	Kingsley.
Cupid's Arrows	Rudyard Kipling.
Venus Annodomini	Rudyard Kipling.
*The Old Familiar Faces	Lamb.
In Nevada ...	Leland.
*King Robert of Sicily	Longfellow.
*The Legend Beautiful	Longfellow.
*The Two Angels	Longfellow.
*The Monk Felix	Longfellow.
*Sandalphon	Longfellow.
*The Norman Baron	Longfellow.
Paul Revere's Ride	Longfellow.
*Beggars	Locker.
'Sir Launfal	Lowell.
'At the Opera	Lytton.
The Wives of Miletus	(*Bulwer*) Lytton.
'The Waking of the Lark	Eric Mackay.
'Beethoven at the Piano	Eric Mackay.

*The Ballad of Sir Aglovaile	*George Macdonald.*
Virginia	*Macaulay.*
Horatius	*Macaulay.*
The Armada	*Macaulay.*
A Chorus on the Alkestis	*Lucas Malet.*
*L'Allegro	*Milton.*
*Paradise and the Peri	*Moore.*
*The Vale of Avoca	*Moore.*
The Editor's Story	*A. Mills.*
*Voices	*Lewis Morris.*
*Marsyas	*Lewis Morris.*
*The Sirens	*William Morris.*
*The Singing of the Magnificat	*E. Nisbet.*
Firenez Rinzi	*E. Nisbet.*
*The Sacristan's Story	*Ouida.*
Our Foreign Relations	*James Payn.*
Our Back Garden	*James Payn.*
Mrs. B.'s Alarms	*James Payn.*
Our Last Lodgings	*James Payn.*
Double Glo'ster	*James Payn.*
Prince	*Harriet Childe-Pemberton.*
*Ode to St. Cecilia's Day	*Pope.*
*The Dying Christian to his Soul	*Pope.*
*The Poet and the Muse	*W. H. Pollock.*
*The Raven	*Edgar Allen Poe.*
*The Bells	*Edgar Allen Poe.*
The Duke's Commission	*Margaret Preston.*
*The Belle of the Ball	*Praed.*
*The County Ball	*Praed.*
Arrivals at a Watering Place	*Praed.*
The Last of the Incas	*Prescott.*
*The Legend of Provence	*Adelaide Anne Procter.*

The Legend of Bregenz	.. *Adelaide Anne Procter.*
*The Angel's Story	.. *Adelaide Anne Procter.*
*The Story of the Faithful Soul	.. *Adelaide Anne Procter.*
*The King's Tragedy	.. *Rossetti.*
*The Blessed Damozel	.. *Rossetti.*
The White Ship	.. *Rossetti.*
Sister Helen	.. *Rossetti.*
Maud Clare	*Christina Rossetti.*
A Royal Princess	*Christina Rossetti.*
*Jessie Cameron	*Christina Rossetti.*
The Clouds	.. *Ruskin.*
Big Tom	*James Runciman.*
*The Cloud	.. *Shelley.*
*Stanzas written in Dejection	.. *Shelley.*
*An Invocation	.. *Shelley.*
*To the Night	.. *Shelley.*
*' Music, when Sweet Voices die '	.. *Shelley.*
Ode to the West Wind	.. *Shelley.*
Ode to the Skylark	.. *Shelley.*
Two Scenes from the *School for Scandal*	*Sheridan.*
Three Scenes from *Hamlet*	*Shakespeare.*
Romeo and the Apothecary	*Shakespeare.*
Henry V. and the Princess	*Shakespeare.*
Henry V. at Agincourt	*Shakespeare.*
Henry IV. and the Prince	*Shakespeare.*
Abdication of Richard II.	*Shakespeare.*
Revolt of the Percies	*Shakespeare.*
The Fall of Wolsey	*Shakespeare.*
*On Music	*Shakespeare.*
*The Last Minstrel	.. *Scott.*
The Death of Marmion	.. *Scott.*
The Abbot's Prophecy	.. *Scott.*

Lochinvar .. .. Scott.
Bonnie Dundee .. .. Scott.
The Stowaway .. .. Clement Scott.
A Passage from John Inglesant .. .. Shorthouse.
The Cataract of Lodore .. .. .. Southey.
*The Knight of Intercession .. .. J. Stone.
*A Match .. .. Swinburne.
*The Brook .. .. Tennyson.
*'Tears, idle Tears' .. .. Tennyson.
*Ode on the Death of the Duke of Wellington Tennyson.
*The Lotus Eaters .. .. Tennyson.
*The Day Dream .. .. Tennyson.
*Amphion .. .. Tennyson.
*Crossing the Bar .. .. Tennyson.
The Revenge .. .. Tennyson.
The Defence of Lucknow .. .. .. Tennyson.
Guinevere .. .. Tennyson.
The Victim .. .. Tennyson.
Scene from *Harold* .. .. Tennyson.
Scene from *Becket* .. .. Tennyson.
Lord Ronald and Lady Clare .. .. Tennyson.
Locksley Hall .. .. Tennyson.
Lady Clara Vere de Vere .. .. .. Tennyson.
The Grandmother .. .. Tennyson.
Charge of the Light Brigade .. .. Tennyson.
The Talking Oak .. .. Tennyson.
Enoch Arden .. .. Tennyson.
*Thou and I .. .. T. Tilton.
*The Blackbird .. .. F. Tennyson.
Scene from *Philip Van Artevelde* .. Sir Henry Taylor.
A Little Dinner at Tymmyns's .. .. Thackeray.
An Incident from *Vanity Fair* .. .. Thackeray.

How to Live Well on Nothing a Year	.. *Thackeray.*
The White Squall	.. *Thackeray.*
The Cane-bottom'd Chair	.. *Thackeray.*
Altruism	.. *R. Trowbridge.*
The Death of the Old Squire ..	*W. Thornbury.*
Underground Jottings	.. *E. Turner.*
My First and Last Appearance ..	.. *E. Turner.*
Pioneers! O Pioneers!	*Walt Whitman.*
*The Singer in the Prison	*Walt Whitman.*
Ode on the Intimations of Immortality	.. *Wordsworth.*
The Witch's Daughter	*Whittier.*
The Amphisbæna	*Whittier.*
*Barbara Frietchie	*Whittier.*
Maud Müller	*Whittier.*
*The Garrison of Cape Ann	*Whittier.*
The Curé's Tale	*A. F. Westmacott.*
The Sword of John Heering of Horn	*A. F. Westmacott.*
A Night with a Stork	.. *C. Wilcox.*
*The Leper	.. *N. P. Willis.*
*Love in a Cottage	.. *N. P. Willis.*
The Hat	.. *M. S.*
Show Sunday	.. *M. S.*
The Wives of Brixham	*M. B. S.*
'Forgive'	.. *Anon.*
Zerviah Hope	.. *Anon.*
*The Muster Roll	.. *Anon.*
The Newsboy's Debt	.. *Anon.*
*Fair Helen	*Old Ballad.*

Etc., Etc., Etc.

* These pieces are recited with music.

Sometimes in my audiences I have seen

people, book in hand, 'following' me line for line in the text. Nothing terrifies me so much. One must possess nerves of iron, or of cotton-wool, to stand such a test. Nothing, too, were I an auditor, would be more tiresome to me than to have to stare at a book when some one was reciting or acting. Surely it is a sadly inartistic, wrongly-applied-educational thing to do. All dramatic emotion, all disengaged imagination, seems impossible under such circumstances. Such people must be born examiners, and ought to belong to the School Board. When you are following a speaker with a finger to the printed line, dramatic action and facial expression are lost, and pauses are nothing more than hindrances. It is a beautiful example of approaching a thing from the wrong point of view. I have been wickedly tempted at such times to put in some wholly naughty, injurious, astounding, bewildering word which would scare and startle the good people into looking up. Only then the fingers would have been pointed at me! It is a case of Sterne's critic counting the length of a pause which Garrick made between certain words by the stop-watch—'Did you not look at him?' 'I looked only at the stop-watch!'

I confess that I cannot get on without applause. I don't think I ever met a dramatic artist worth his salt who could. Without it one gets chilled. Applause is not only as wine to one's courage and enthusiasm, but it is something not unlike a sip of wine to one's throat and voice. The little moments of pause and rest thus gained are a positive physical help— at least, they are to me.

Then, too, I am sure that if an audience is thoroughly pleased and impressed, it will applaud. I do not believe in the pretty amateurish compliment, that if people are very deeply moved they cannot applaud, and that sometimes silence is the best expression of an audience's satisfaction, etc. Toward all such grandiloquent statements I am tempted to become childishly rude, and use that foolish but unanswerable word—Fiddle! There may, indeed, be a momentary pause whilst an audience recovers its breath, as it were, but then the applause will burst out the louder. If I do not get applause, no amount of sophistry from myself or from others will convince me that I have other than failed. To a few persons of deep feeling and small professional experience it may seem jarring to applaud when they are greatly moved. It may not occur to them to do so. But I am glad to say these are exceptional cases. For myself, however deeply I am moved at a performance, I never lose the double sense of personal emotion and critical enjoyment in the performance as a work of art. I never for a moment lose that, or my observation of the execution and method employed to raise the emotion. I do not want to do so. It would be to lose half the pleasure. If I lost this sense, any appeals of pathos, terror, or pity would be painful, instead of being, as with it they are, the most refined and delicate enjoyment and satisfaction. In this matter, however, the mass of an audience are true in feeling—as they are in most matters. The applause rings out at the right moment. If it does not, there is failure in the art somewhere.

As a rule I have found people both kind and imaginative in my work in private rooms. There must be, of course, a good deal for every artist to put up with on occasions which are constructed, not artistically, but socially. Whether the custom which obtains in these days of bringing artistic entertainment into social intercourse is a desirable one may be open to question, both from the point of view of art and of society. But, however well the combination may be carried out, it is inevitable that the artist will meet with various disturbing and defeating elements.

The conditions of a private entertainment are radically different from those which govern a public performance; and the audience listens from a different and, I fear I must add, a lower level. The general idea would be, doubtless, that a drawing-room would require and appreciate more delicate and refined pieces than a public hall. I accepted this idea when I started in my work. But I soon learned it was a mistake. Drawing-rooms require broader and not more delicate work than public assemblies. They fidget and yawn over pieces to which a shilling gallery would listen with rapt attention. To give such poems as Milton's *L'Allegro*, Tennyson's *Lotus Eaters*, Shelley's *Cloud*, or Byron's *Isles of Greece*, in a drawing-room is to court lack of attention. No; it requires something far more elementary and 'dramatic'—something where the colour is laid on with a heavy brush, and the sentiment gives you a good hard knock. 'I like to be curdled,' said a great lady to me, during my first season; 'I like that piece about a costermonger and his dog: and that piece where a child is run over by a train. . . . Oh, isn't it run over? . . . Well, you think it's going to be, and that is nearly as good!' 'Don't you recite anything about a good murder?' was the question, accompanied with a gracious and sunny smile, that was put to me on an occasion when negatives are somewhat difficult.

Of course drawing-rooms differ as much as public audiences, and there are notable exceptions to every rule. But, whilst gratefully acknowledging the invariable courtesy and kindness I have received, I must own that, from a point of art, private audiences must not be weighed in any very exacting scales, or they will be found wanting. Their attention generally does more honour to their heart than to their head. But what would you have? We can none of us be two things at once. Guest and auditor are two very distinct parts. Their claims and duties often clash sadly. And, after all, on these occasions, with everybody present the first *rôle* is that of the guest.

In my own public recitals in London, everything is thought over, and every possibility of jarring circumstance, and of unnecessary appeal to self-consciousness, is, as far as may

PRIVATE ENTERTAINMENTS. 45

be, guarded against. But all this is impossible in a private room, even when every courtesy and kindness is shown. The piano is a 'dark continent,' and often proves a field of defeat. The audience is generally so close that I cannot do them the greatest kindness and pay them the best compliment an artist can—namely, forget them. I must remember that they are all guests of a hostess, and that the occasion is one of social intercourse. It is true an artist is justified in protecting his work from injury, that he should never fail to do so; but he must also protect his hostess from annoyance. If he accepts a position he must accept its conditions and limitations.

It seems discourteous and ungrateful to remember and record the little annoyances and absurdities of my private work, and not also name the many pleasant points; especially when it is true to say that the pleasant points have been numerous, and the annoyances few and far between. But then, the pleasantnesses are like virtues on the stage—rather tame to contemplate. It is of the little irregularities that we like to hear. From time to time odd things happen and are said to a public artist at private entertainments. I have no tale of rudeness or discourtesy to tell. I have heard such from fellow-artists, but I must in truth say I have met nothing but kind consideration and perfect courtesy in my work. Still, as I said, odd things come into one's experience. A few of these I will venture to name. 'The rest is silence.'

1. I was giving a recital one afternoon at Lady D——'s, in Portman Square. Amongst other pieces I gave the well-known *King Robert of Sicily*, by Longfellow. Mrs. Duncan Stewart was sitting close in front. She was always an enthusiastic listener, and as she had seen and heard all the best public artists of her day, her enthusiasm was a compliment worth receiving. At the end of the poem, she started up, raised her hand over her head, and said, 'I'm for the king! I'm for the king! And so, my dear Mr. Clifford Harrison, I'm sure are you, from the way you spoke his words. I'm for the king! It was a most unjustifiable proceeding. Don't talk to me about angels! Shameful! For what was his fault after all, poor dear man? Nothing! a little pardonable petulance at a tedious service! Why, it might happen to any of us!'

2. Some time ago I had put down Mrs. Browning's *The Dead Pan* in a programme for

a private recital in Queen's Gate. It was rather rash, but I thought the audience would be above the average. I was going to begin the poem, when I heard a lady near me say quite distinctly, 'What is the next piece? Something funny, I hope. Oh yes—I see— *The Dead Pan.* Dear me, how odd! Of course it's funny; something about bad cooking, I suppose'!

In one week I received two criticisms that greatly pleased me. In both instances the critic was a lady of position. The first was on Miss Procter's *Faithful Soul;* the second on Miss Jean Ingelow's *High Tide on the Coast of Lincolnshire.* I must hope that the poems are well known, in which case the following criticisms will be appreciated.

1. 'What an entertaining thing that was you gave us last night at Mrs. ——'s, about a poor woman who was away somewhere—somewhere abroad, I think. No, perhaps she was dead; but at any rate she had gone away; and then she came back to look after her husband, and found he was quite happy and had married again! So like a man! I thought that was very good. I don't know when I've been more entertained. We had a good laugh over

it at home to-day! Dear Mr. Harrison, come and see us soon!'

2. 'But of all the pieces you recited, the one I liked by far the best, don't you know—though, of course, all were quite charming—but the one I liked the best was that piece about Queen Elizabeth. Yes. Don't you remember? Yes, you must. There was a poor girl in it—Jetty, I think was her name! And she was drowned, don't you know. Quite too sad. But it was all beautiful; and the music! How odd you don't remember! Ah yes— yes, I thought you would. But I knew it was in the reign of Elizabeth, because the name was constantly referred to—" Elizabeth—Elizabeth!" Though I don't at all agree that a " sweeter woman ne'er drew breath." Yes, it quite excited me. But then, that's what I always say about your recitations, don't you know. They *are* so stimulating to one's imagination'! Evidently.

There is an admirable candour about some great ladies. 'Mr. Harrison, I don't think I shall ask you to recite for me this season,' said Lady —— of —— to me one day. 'I have heard you several times, and I get so tired of people. I like something new.'

When I first appeared as a reciter, it was she who said, 'I like Mr. Clifford Harrison's recitals so much,—on account of the pauses, you know.'

I had a curious experience at a private recital one afternoon in the season of 1887. That May and June, I recollect, were fruitful in such matters. On the occasion I refer to, I had, to begin with, a good deal of difficulty in finding the house, up beyond Regent's Park. When at last I got there, I saw no sort of sign of a party. The signs are numerous, and vary according to the social status of the party-giver. I thought I was pretty well versed in all these signs; but absolutely none could be read into the very unreceptive-looking house before me. I rang the bell. A neat but severe servant answered the door. I asked if Mrs. A—— lived there. 'Yes.' But the monosyllable was given with none of the 'open-locks-whoever-knocks' air of a servant who knows that her mistress is 'at home.' On the contrary, this neat, severe woman seemed to bar entrance. I had to ask if there was not a party there, and to give my name. Then she said, 'Yes. It's all right.' I went in. The house was silent. I put my hat in a little room, where

I found another neat, severe woman, half buried in hats and things, and solemnly labelling them with numbers. The hats and things seemed to argue the presence of heads; and on inquiry, I was told, 'Yes; everybody is here and waiting!' Yet I heard no voices, no footsteps, no reassuring tinkle of cup and tea spoon. I became nervous. It was like a dream. I was ushered upstairs, and the drawing-room door was thrown open. Yes, it was true. Clearly everybody was there; the room was full. But there was no noise, no unseemly bustle. It was all very quiet, very expectant, very observant. It was more than ever like a dream. My name was not announced; but an old lady, with an exuberant and disorganized sort of cap, came forward quickly, and said 'Oh yes. It's Mr. Clifford Harrison. That's quite right. We are all ready. I shall be glad if you will begin.'

It was a curious assembly. There were old ladies in black satin and large brooches; men in lavender kid gloves; a few young ladies and some children, who nudged each other, and evidently regarded me as something funny and phenomenal, and with regret that I wasn't dissolving views. One of the young ladies sang—really nicely. One of the men in lavender kids whistled. And an old gentleman played with his daughter that very terrible duet, whereof the 'secondo' is an alternation of the common chords, and the 'primo' (he was 'primo') an exhibition of how to transform two fingers into sticks and a musical instrument into a toy.

It was four o'clock when I began, and everybody had been there a quarter of an hour. It was half-past seven when I left off, and everybody was still there. Furthermore, as I was going away, I met tea and ices going upstairs for the old ladies who did not care to move. The guests were very quiet and subdued; but the hostess was possessed with an excitement so great that it magnetized, so to speak, her very cap, which continually seemed of its own free will to stand up on end. Whenever I ended a recitation, and there was a buzz of applause, the hostess said, 'Oh, thank you very much, I'm sure! We're all—er.'

She was most kind and solicitous for all her guests' comfort, including mine. But the dreamlike effect of the whole affair was accentuated when she said, 'And now I wish you would recite that piece which I heard you give once, about a dear little girl who went to see a poor old man, and was caught up in the sails of a windmill, and they couldn't stop it, but she wasn't hurt a bit. I don't think I was ever so impressed. Would you mind giving that piece?' It was in vain that I assured her —that I assured myself—that I had never recited any such piece, knew no such piece, had never heard of any such piece. She maintained the fact that I had recited it, and that she had been present, and had never been so impressed, and would I give it then?

The dream positively rose to nightmare, when at last, coming downstairs on my way out, I heard my hostess—in answer to a lady who, with a curiosity which I felt to be a compliment, had asked her whether I was married—say, 'Oh, dear me, yes! Of course! And has a dear little boy who plays the violin.'

I did not feel awake until I got into the hansom, and was driving home.

—'Yes; well, I'm sure we're all very much obliged to you, Mr. Harrison, for these beautiful poems and things. I'm sorry to interrupt you in the middle of the programme.'—(It was our host who was speaking to me, at a rather crowded party in Kensington; summer-time;

small garden illuminated with 'fairy lamps;' and a marquee for ices, etc., etc.—everything very smart). 'But I didn't quite know how serious and all that sort of thing your entertainment was. I thought it was comical. Can't you 'liven us up a bit? Sing us a good song. Can't you do that? Like Grossmith and Corney Grain.' (I regretted my inability.) 'Why, Grossmith imitates you! Why don't you imitate him?' (Again I expressed regret.) 'Well, I don't know what's to be done. If I wasn't so busy myself, seeing after everybody, I'd sing a song myself.' (I invited the trial.) 'No, I can't just yet. But do, for goodness' sake, make us laugh.' (I promised to try.) 'That's right. And pitch the poetry overboard. Never mind the programme. Make 'em laugh!'

I really quite sympathized with him. I often feel that laughter is the best, is the right, note for these occasions. I made it sound then, and the host was delighted. When he heard the first hearty laugh, he looked in at the door, and waved a smiling approval to me. 'But,' he said, when I was going away, ' I shall never forget those first two pieces. Oh lor! I thought we were all in church! It was too bad of you. Well, you made up for it after. But I *was* frightened. Good night.'

The terror some hosts and hostesses have of recitations that may be too dramatic or pathetic has often afforded me amusement, and made selection of pieces difficult. But the terror is, after all, a reasonable one; for it cannot be denied that reciters have sadly affected pieces of the livid and lugubrious description. Yet a recital, even in private, which entirely eliminates pathos will be as dull as one that has no relief of humour. And I have noticed that people who have an unconscionable dread of pathos have also a very slight sense of humour.

'I hope that none of the recitations this evening will be *too* dramatic, Mr. Harrison. Nothing to affect the feelings too much. Some people are coming who are so extraordinarily sensitive. So please—please be careful of our feelings!'

After that opening speech, for example, from my hostess one evening, I knew what to expect, viz.—no feelings to be careful of! My expectations were realized. People who have swift and true 'feelings'—artistic feelings, I mean, which will answer the call of imagination —like to have them appealed to. They would, in fact, consider any performance which did not appeal to them a poor thing in the way of art. But people who have a very attenuated supply of these same artistic feelings, like to guard the slender stock carefully; and when they have to expend any of it, they do not enjoy the outlay.

So, on the evening I have referred to, we were all to be hopelessly sprightly. But, alas! from lack of contrast and variety, the sprightliness lost colour and point; and, as I expected, my hostess and her friends who were so extraordinarily sensitive had but small receptive power of humour, even when Thackeray or George Eliot presented it to them. The whole evening on that occasion, in truth, might be described in the words my housekeeper employed one day in telling me about a recital given by a new young aspirant to fame whom she went to hear, 'Well, you know, sir, I dare say it was all very good and that; but it was quiet, and it was very long, and I wasn't altogether sorry when it was over. It wasn't funny, you know, sir, and it wasn't deep. I didn't laugh; neither did I cry.'

Another recital of the same kind fell to my lot a few days afterwards. Our hostess on this occasion also was an old lady of deplorably cheerful disposition. She seemed to regard everybody as a standing joke. I have a theory that anything excessive is purchased at the price of somebody's loss. There is only so much vitality, laughter, energy, feeling; and any one who absorbs and assimilates more than his share of these elements robs other folks. I know people of such exuberant vitality that they positively fatigue me to be with them. They take something out of the air and leave me the weaker. Any one who laughs overmuch depresses me abominably. Our hostess of the night in question possessed a cheerfulness that gave us the heartache.

She told me at once that she hoped I wasn't going to recite anything dramatic, or pathetic, or poetic; but only funny pieces. 'It's all for fun, you know,' she said; 'just for fun. I hate and detest pathos and sentiment. It's so silly! I haven't common patience with it all!'

This seemed to me a bad beginning—but worse remained behind. It was useless for me to argue the point at issue, as to the silliness of sentiment; and of course I said I would give pieces as far as possible of a humorous and light kind. I really wondered why she had engaged me at all. The programme had been arranged and printed. But I substituted comedy for all the graver pieces —a good deal to some of my auditors' disappointment, I think.

One poem, however, she insisted on having, —some one had just told her it was 'beautiful'— Longfellow's *Legend Beautiful*. I pointed out to her that it was one of the gravest pieces I recited, involving suggestions and thoughts of the highest and deepest kind, being, in fact, a legend of the Beatific vision. I told her that I seldom gave it in a private room, as, although I do not shrink from the claims of pathos and drama, I do shrink from what seems lacking in timely reverence. But it was no use. 'You can put it in after *Underground Jottings*,' she said. 'It doesn't matter; I don't mind. It's only for fun, after all.'

I prefaced the recitation with a few words of apology and preparation, saying I had been specially asked to give the piece, and that I hoped it would not seem too clashing as . . . 'All right!' said the irrepressible old lady, cutting my explanation short—'all right! Let's hear it! It's all for fun! Only for fun!'

Truly, it takes all sorts to make a world, and a funny world at that!

There is no doubt that, for any thing connected with entertainment, humour must be 'up to date.' Literary humour has a different standpoint. But humour is, practically, a varying quantity, and, like good taste in dress, or in decoration, is a thing each generation grows for itself. The humour of a bygone generation sounds as old-fashioned as the coat of the humourist would look in a modern assembly. I was saying this one afternoon to Lord Aberdare,—who had been suggesting to me for recitation Swift's verse describing how he fancies his friends would receive the news of his death (it was at Lady Knutsford's, then Lady Holland, that it occurred),—when humour was unexpectedly illustrated practically to us. For Lord Houghton came in during the afternoon, having been at a smart wedding. He promptly went to sleep. Morpheus was confessed alike to eye and ear of those around. But at the end of one of the pieces he started up, came to me, vowed it was the best thing he had ever heard, asked me who was the author, and where it was published. It was his own *Story of Prince Emelius.*

In another grade of society—at a pleasant, hearty, suburban party—humour of a grim kind was illustrated the next evening to me.

There was a regular sit-down supper of the old-fashioned kind after the recital. The host was the kindest and the most excitable of men. He had a curiously red face, and a lot of white hair all round it, like a figure I have seen in a Jack-in-the-box. He seemed positively ablaze with excitement. I shall never forget him at supper-time. I was taken in, and given the place of honour next to the hostess—a charming old lady. I had to catch the last train back to town, and a 'fly' to take me to the station was announced as being at the door. I suppose this started the idea of hurry in the excellent man's mind. At any rate, he exhibited an ever-increasing agitation and expedition. In vain his wife and daughters tried to pacify him. It was evident they were used to such scenes, and dreaded them. But their appeals for calmness were all in vain. He carved, hacked, hewed, tore into shreds the turkey before him. He heaped plate after plate, till the waiters had to range them on the sideboard. Pieces of agitated turkey and truffles flew on to the tablecloth, and almost into the laps of the discomfited guests near him. In vain his placid wife kept saying 'Thank you, dear Henry, that's enough. Keep calm.'—'We have all got plenty of time, my love.'—'Let me entreat you, Henry, to sit down.'—'Induce your father to sit down Alice.'—'We are all quite calm.'—'Henry pray don't cut any more.'—'John, take the turkey away from your master!'

The wretched bird was at length carried off; and then he called for boiled fowls, tongue ham, anything—'Only let us get on!' he cried. 'Plenty of time,' she replied from the end of the table. 'My dear Henry, nobody is in a hurry. Let us all keep quite quiet!'

He gave me the kindest and most cordial of good nights and thanks; and I left him distributing jelly wildly to everybody within arm's reach, and filling up indiscriminate glasses with the excellent champagne.

The lack of the sense of humour is beautifully exemplified in a letter I once received. It was the climax to many odd letters from people anent my work. It was from a lady at whose 'At Home' I was to have recited the former season. Unluckily I was ill on that occasion—had lost my voice, and could not recite. Of course it was a tiresome business for her, as for me. The following season she wrote again to ask me to recite at her party. But, not unnaturally, she was a little nervous after the last year's disappointment. She wrote in the third person, and was certainly singular. 'Mrs. A. must request, if Mr. Clifford Harrison accepts this engagement, that nothing whatever is allowed to interfere with its fulfilment. Last year Mrs. A. suffered a good deal of inconvenience from Mr. Harrison's illness, and she must request that, if Mr. Harrison is ill this year, he will *give her at least a week's notice.*'

But, as I said, many odd letters have fallen to my portion—letters which greatly cheered and enlivened the crowded road of correspondence. I was once in communication with a lady about a recital at her house in the north. Between anxiety that all should go well, and a desire not to overstep the limits of assured statement of a certain religious school, her letters afforded food for contemplation. 'Can you,' she wrote—'can you *promise positively* and *without fail* to recite here (*D. V.*) on the 23rd of next month?'

Carlyle, I believe, was amused at this formula in a letter from a great lady who promised to come, D.V., to see him on a certain day. 'Ah!' he said, recalling the many occasions when she had promised to come and had never appeared—'Ah! but most unfortunately D. never does V.!'

I remember quoting the letter I had received to a parson whom I met at a country house. But, alas for me! he failed to see the humour and only scented irreverence; and his anxious and manifold inquiries as to the exact nature, verbal and otherwise, of the recitations, each and every, I was going to give that evening in his parish school-house, struck to my ears the note of humour he had failed to perceive in my quotation. He was only reassured when I told him that it was one of my chief aims in the choice of pieces for recitation to avoid anything that could, in fairness, be considered irreverent.

At recitals in country houses the parsons of the neighbourhood are always gathered together. As a rule they make a most excellent and appreciative portion of the audience.

But when many parsons are present I know that one thing will happen—I shall be asked where certain recitations are to be found. Parsons have no conscience in this matter.

A FORM OF CATECHISM. 63

Once, at a large party where the cloth was very conspicuous, two parsons came up and asked me about *Our Eye-witness on the Ice*, *Jupiter and Co.*, *Sheltered*, a piece of Longfellow's, and two stories of my own. One of the gentlemen went further: he offered me his note-book and pencil, and coolly said, 'Kindly write down the necessary information.' I suppose I looked surprised. I did not take the note-book and pencil. He went on to tell me that he wasted so much time in looking for things—often fruitlessly—to read at village entertainments. 'I have sometimes spent two hours,' he said irritably, 'in searching for a piece.' I told him I could well believe it: one of the recitations he asked for had given me a search of three months, and a good deal of expense in purchasing books, etc. I went on to explain that the requests for information, verbally and by letter, about recitations were so numerous—often four and five a week—that I had to make a definite rule on the subject. To grant one request and refuse another would be impossible; to grant all would go far to cheapen and lower the interest of nearly every recitation I gave. The novelty of a recitation is more than half its value. 'I am sure,' I said, 'that you will see the position and pardon me.' 'Certainly,' he replied. Then, after a slight pause, and a cough, he offered the pencil and note-book again, and said quite pleasantly, ' Then *will* you kindly write down the necessary information—the names of the books and the respective publishers, if you please ? '

What is one to say to, or do with, people like this ?

On such occasions one has to take the point of view of humour. But sometimes it is rather difficult at the time. I can distinctly recall one occasion when I found it difficult to do so, although that point of view was an obvious one.

It was a day given over to the making of ropes of sand. By date it was December 22, 1886. It is a humiliating chronicle of mistake; but as it is the only one my work of these many years has to show, I do not mind confessing to it. I went all the way to Hull for a recital at an Institute—and recital there was none. It was a phantom—a mirage. It is unnecessary to narrate how the mistake arose —in chief part it was mine. The words ' Hull, recital, Institute,' had never been erased in my book of engagements. I had positively refused

an engagement for the day, thinking I was due
at Hull. Some doubt crossed me, as I could
find no definite letters. A voice suggested a
telegram; I silenced the voice, and started. It
was a bitterly cold day, and Hull is a long way.
Five hours in the train was a tedious journey.
I drove straight to the Institute. Dark and
silent. Not a lecture night. I drove to the
President's. The interview was civil but
painful. He regretted, and I regretted. He
was most courteous, and said he was dreadfully
distressed; I was most untruthful, and said I
did not mind it much. He asked me to dine
and stay the night; but I preferred to end the
dark business at once. I went to an hotel,
dined, and read a novel of Gaborieau's. I
started back for town at eight o'clock. I
arrived in London at 2.40. I learnt new
recitations on the way, and declaimed *Sister
Helen* to myself, until I was colder with
terror than with frost. I told myself it was
altogether an amusing incident; but philosophy
gave way when, on arriving at Finsbury Park,
I could not find my ticket, and had to pay the
fare again. A slow hansom landed me at my
door at 3.15. I had travelled, and been hatted
and cloaked (save for a brief while at dinner)

for fifteen hours; and the outing cost me nearly five pounds.

To arrive on the day after the fair is infuriating; on the day before the fair is humiliating; but to arrive on the day when there is no fair, never was to be a fair, when the fair has been utterly abolished and done away with, is an experience that perhaps is unique.

Another occasion on which I found the point of view of humour difficult, though not unattainable even at the time, was at a memorable recital at Oxford, in the April of 1880. remember that I went to the beautiful city for this occasion with peculiar interest. It was the first time I had recited there. My love for Oxford has always been very great. Perhaps its meadows and uplands remind me of Henley; perhaps in a former incarnation was at college there. At least it is certain that the very names Oxford, Iffley, Cumnor, are beautiful to me, and seem to possess memories I love. I was once here for two months sketching. It was a delightful time. I used to begin the day by saying over to myself Matthew Arnold's *Scholar Gypsy*. The present Dean of Westminster and Mrs. Bradley were very kind to me. It was altogether a pleasant episode. I went to give my first recital there with peculiar interest and pleasant anticipation.

It was a great function. Prince Leopold was staying at the Deanery. Oxford was bidden to meet him in Christchurch Hall. The beautiful building was prettily decorated. Between the hours of 'Hall' and of the party, a great transformation had been effected, converting the dining-hall into the reception-room. A band was stationed in the 'quad.' Miss Hopekirk was to play; I was to recite. Down each side of the hall were refreshment-tables, nobly spread for the continual feast of those assembled. All Oxford came *en grande tenue*. It was really a pretty sight—from one point of view. Some eight hundred people or more were present, I suppose. There were no seats, save chairs for the Royal party at the Deanery.

The result was inevitable—a Babel of voice and a clink of teaspoon and teacup. The collected voice of Oxford is as the sound of many waters. The Prince was very gracious to me. 'I fear,' he said, 'you must find it difficult to recite under these circumstances.' I owned that the circumstances were stronger

than I. He asked me to recite my own lines
—*The Signalman*—of which he said he had
heard. I gave the piece, and positively almost
gained a hearing. It is depressing to think
one may at such times—as experience has now
unanswerably proved to me—recite Tennyson,
Browning, and Milton, and nobody will listen;
and rant out a piece like *The Signalman* and
gain a hushed attention. Even Oxford accorded to Melodrama the hearing it denied to
Poetry. I could not help comparing the recital
that night with those I had given on the afternoon and evening of the previous day. In the
afternoon it was at a middle-class party in the
suburbs; in the evening at a Working-man's
Institute; both gave me audiences of perfect
sympathy. No point of pathos or humour was
missed. I was able to give Browning's *Saul*,
and Tennyson's *Lotus Eaters*, and Milton's
L'Allegro, a passage from *Vanity Fair*, and a
piece of Austin Dobson's. And yet it is really
unfair to compare the occasions. They were
different in kind. The Oxford audience under
the same conditions would have been as good
as, and perhaps better than, those audiences
of the day before. Had I been one of my own
auditors in Christchurch Hall, I should have

voted myself a bore, and joined the chorus of conversation and tinkled a teacup. A certain dual-personality enabled me to review the situation with amusement as well as occupy it with—the reverse. Professor Max Müller said to me when it was all over, and I had the feeling of having been beaten with sticks many and thick, 'What can you think of Oxford? Are we not "young barbarians at play"? But I can assure you when I came in I had no idea that anything was going on until Mrs. Max Müller said, ".There's Mr. Clifford Harrison! I believe he is reciting."'

The Dean and Mrs. Liddell were most courteous and kind; but the thanks I received, and which were so cordially given, were sadly undeserved.

That was the second time I have wished that I was a string band.

The walk back to the beautiful 'High' was wonderfully refreshing, and I recited Matthew Arnold's lines and made myself a most sympathetic audience.

What a blessed thing is the point of view of humour!

The night after that recital at Oxford, I remember I was due to recite at W——, a small country town east of London. I was recommended by Mr. Rice (a stationer and bookseller in the High Street, who had organized the recital) to go to the Saracen's Head. Thither I went to dress and to dine. I got a room, and unpacked my things. I then discovered that there was no dress waistcoat in the portmanteau. It was bad, but it might have been worse. I rang the bell, and looked critically at the landlord, who answered it. But no; *that* was impossible. So I asked him to send out and scour the town for something that would do. He returned soon with boxes of white waistcoats. They were morning waistcoats, and of curious 'cut;' but I selected one, and knowing certain 'dodges' of the theatrical dressing-room, by the aid of a few pins and a little manipulation, I made it more or less fit me and the occasion. I went down to dinner. A good commercial gentleman was in the coffee-room. He was minded to be loquacious. The book I laid open at my side to read did not daunt him.

'Giving a sort of entertainment here, a'n't you?'

'Yes.'

'What d'ye call it? Reading? Penny

Reading? Sixpenny Reading? Shilling ditto? Arf Hours with the Poets? What d'ye call it?'

I called it a recital.

'Oh! *That*' (pointing to the shirt front and white waistcoat, and closing one' eye with obtrusive meaning) '*that* ought to bring 'em in!'

A bow from me.

'Will it run to a full room, d'ye think?'

No; I thought it would not run to more than half a full room, if that; as I did not think I was known there.

'Then why did you come? What made you give the thing at all? Why don't you give it up?"

I explained that it was not my speculation.

'Good,' he said; 'I'm with you there! That's yer sort! Who runs it, then?'

Mr. Rice, of the High Street, was arranging it.

'Oh! rough on old Rice, ain't it? I know him. Safe as the bank! 'Ow did he 'ear of you?'

I did not know. Presumably through the papers.

'Oh! I 'ear that Lady —— and party will be there to-night.'

I thought it was likely.

'My! Fancy! I shall go too. No wonder you sported a white waistcoat! I didn't mean to go, but now I've 'ad this talk with yer I shall.'

One day, when I came back to town from a recital overnight at Brighton, I found a Mr. Z—— awaiting my arrival. He had come to talk over an entertainment—to be called 'In Poet-Land'—a series of songs and recitations to be given partly 'in character.' The scene was to be a 'set,' like a stage scene, and was to represent 'In the Clouds;' which was sufficiently vague, and not very complimentary to Poet-Land. The music was his own composition. He had set several well-known poems; he played and sang them to me. I was to recite *The Charge of the Light Brigade* 'in character,' dressed, as he said—with a convenient vagueness suitable to the cloudy nature of the scene—'as a soldier, in a sort of cavalry uniform, with a sword.' I was also to recite Collins's *Ode to the Passions*, attired in Greek costume; 'like,' he added, with a still greater cloudiness of idea and expression—'like a Muse.' Finally, I was, in Highland costume, but shrouded in a military cloak, which was to be thrown aside at the words 'Havelock's glorious Highlanders,' to recite Tennyson's *Defence of Lucknow*, with a view of Lucknow in the distance (magic lantern effect) and an invisible bagpipe playing *The Campbells are coming*. The effect, he was assured, would be 'immense.' He proposed a tour for the provinces and the United States. I did not, however, see my way to accepting the offer.

Yet it was an attempt, though not a felicitous one, to supply a need in recitals from the popular standpoint—I mean the appeal to the eye. With a large section of people who go to entertainments this appeal is, after all, the first consideration.

At the recital which I gave at Bolton one night, a man came into the cheap seats at the back of the hall whilst I was reciting. He looked at the platform and at me with evident strong disapproval. He attracted my attention. I became conscious of little grumblings, and of observations in a detrimental tone of voice. At last Mr. H—— went to the back of the hall and sat down near to the man. The man was muttering to himself (as I was told afterwards), 'Shut up! Shut up! Enough "jaw!" Show is summat!' On being remonstrated with, he said, 'He's not what 'e represents hisself as bein'. Where's the entertainment? He's shown us nowt!' This he repeated again and again in so angry a tone that at last he had to be escorted out, and, with his money returned, asked to go away. But to the last we heard him exclaiming, 'More he 'as! He's shown us nowt! He's shown us nowt! I don't call that a entertainment!' I rather sympathized with him.

For there can be no doubt that the appeal to the eye is recognized and responded to by all who behold it, whilst that to the ear is often a vain and a fond thing, falling on ground which is strangely unreceptive. Even amongst so-called cultivated people the appeal to hearing is often one that obtains a very slight answer. I have often wished that my work permitted me a stronger appeal to the eye than that which lies merely in descriptive action. I have been often amused to watch people, at private parties, to whom the appeal to the ear is one that is not largely recognized, and who have been lured by society and an invitation card into becoming part of an audience. In private, of course, such people are often met with by an artist. Voluntarily they would never go to a mere recital. In public work, therefore, this unsympathetic element in the audience is happily non-existent, but in private it forms a distinct portion of most audiences.

I have never forgotten one lady—very charming in appearance and manner—at an afternoon party in London. She was seated exactly opposite me. She preserved all through the recital the gravity of a South Sea idol. Eyes had she, and pretty ones—yet, metaphorically, she saw not; ears certainly were there, with a diamond in each—neat, shell-like ears too, but they were no indices of hearing. Vacuity sat enthroned on her charming face. Such steadfastness of purpose really amused me to watch. One wondered what world it was she was denizen of. To such there must be, one would fancy, a good deal of the negative in life. But then closed doors are safe.

Once only a ray of intelligence, and realization of the meaning of the words spoken, crossed her face. Browning did it. I was reciting his *Pied Piper*, and when I came to the lines

'. . . To see the people suffer so
From vermin, was a pity;'

at the word 'vermin' she looked slowly round

at her friend with a sort of mute appeal and surprise, as of one who was not accustomed to hear such a word in society. She had never met it 'out' before. That was the only appeal to the ear which apparently gained an answer.

Yet one can never tell. Perhaps she entered into it all. I once saw an old gentleman sitting in the front row of the stalls at one of my recitals, who seemed depressed and annoyed beyond all reason—even in the matter of entertainment. He held his hand permanently over his eyes, as if he were in pain, or in church, —or, peradventure, sleeping. Only twice did he look up, and then he frowned distinctly at me, said something to his companion, and shook his head as if in the strongest disapproval and condemnation. I was quite upset. Yet the next morning I had a letter from him, bearing a name that gave peculiar value to the praise it contained. 'I have heard,' he wrote, 'and seen' (he positively said 'seen!') 'every reciter of note in my life, and I cannot refrain from telling you that I found a satisfaction and fulness of enjoyment in your recital which,' —etc.

After that, whenever I saw any one looking exceptionally bored, I took heart of grace.

I have, however, had recitals which no heart of grace could help me to consider other than hours of trial. Chief amongst these stands the recital at a certain large and famous public school.

Various things worked against me. Thackeray, in his *White Squall*, talks of

'The cabin snoring
With universal nose;'

and certainly I might say that my audience that night coughed with universal throat. And as four-fifths of the audience were boys, the portentous character of the noise may be imagined. I have heard an anecdote told, how that at a theatre one night, during some very pathetic scene, the audible signs of emotion were so great, and accompanied, as usual, by such varieties of nasal publication, that an old gentleman in the pit, wishing not to lose a word of the performance, got in a temper, and at last exclaimed loudly, 'Drat your noses, hold your tongues!' I felt somewhat minded so to exclaim that night. It was hopeless to speak through the noise. Even to make one's self heard would have taxed lungs of iron, and dramatic effect was impossible. Silence—the first and last necessity for effective artistic recitation—was denied. Out of this denial, therefore, grew inattention and want of imagination. Then, naturally, there slowly arose, as the evening went on, an undercurrent of whispered talk amongst the boys. It rose like an invisible sea. I sank. I did not even struggle. When reciting sinks to the 'mere effort to make oneself heard through a noise, I retire from the inglorious lists. I have no unwillingness to attempt the task of making myself heard when it is a mere question of space—the area of a large building. That is an artistic and skilful thing to do, and must be considered a true part of a public speaker's work. But that is wholly and radically different to 'speaking through a noise.' The only way to combat a noise is to whisper—whisper with every appearance of saying something very valuable! The audience will then hush itself into attention, as a rule. That night was an exception, however, to this rule.

It was a trying two hours, every way. Some five hundred people at least were present. So there were, I computed, some five hundred opinions the following day that I was presumably the worst reciter that has ever been—not heard, for I wasn't—but put up on a platform, even in these days when platforms are only less numerous than the reciters who want to mount them.

After such a night as that I have recorded, it was pleasant to come back to London to my exceptionally bright and enthusiastic audiences at the Steinway Hall. An old playgoer—a man of great observation and experience—once told me he had never seen an audience more quick and responsive than that which so generously gathered round me at my own recitals.

Often, too, I have found delightfully hearty audiences amongst the Working-men's Institutes and in London Parish Rooms. One of the pleasantest recitals I ever gave was in Toynbee Hall, when an entertainment had been organized by Mrs. Robert Willis. There was an excellent feast of good things, and I was to recite Dickens's *Christmas Carol*. There was nothing stinted in the measure of appreciation and enjoyment given to the story and the telling. It was a night of generous feeling. One felt that Charles Dickens lived again for the time being in the hearts of those who listened; those who laughed and cried, and felt the better alike for smiles and tears.

Another such occasion I recall in St. Giles's

Schools. The big schoolroom was crammed. The atmosphere was something that could be felt. It would be sentimentality to say that I prefer such an audience to one of cultivated people. Artistically, it is often coarse in touch, and blind to the finer appeals. But there is great heartiness within its own scope of feeling, and what it feels it feels generously, and does not apologize for. As the recital went on, the wits got clearer, and the artistic sense was quickened. I always allowed time after any 'telling' line for the buzz and flutter of understanding that was sure to follow. For I knew by experience that nearly everybody would turn round to his or her neighbour, and repeat and explain it, although very probably the neighbour had heard it quite as well as the repeater, and was busy in turn repeating it to some one else.

As usual on such occasions, the best pieces went the best. I did not try, of course, any of the higher flights of poetry; but still I gave them pieces of distinct literary value and poetic thought. It is curious to note how far afield one may venture with such an audience. It is the greatest mistake to try to come down to what some people might call their level; to think you will please them by giving them stories of their own rank of life and tales of every day. Unless such stories are told by a master hand, they will utterly fail to hit the right mark. For the points where the characters and the phraseology are untrue to life are detected at once. Pieces of sentimentality that delight a drawing-room — about beggar boys, and 'costers,' and hospitals, and alleys—have to confess their bathos before an audience in St. Giles's. They are recognized at once, ruthlessly and with keen insight, as not being true to life. Such an audience likes to be lifted out of itself. It likes to hear of beauty, and heroism, and grandeur. Even when it wholly fails to understand, it is willing to surrender itself to the pleasure of feeling glorified. It likes what it calls 'a deep piece.' The shallow pleasure of bald intelligibility is poor in its mind by the side of a vague bright sense of something beyond and above it, something ideal and illuminating. Of course one must not strain this feeling too much; one must have a conscience in the matter. But it is safe to count on the audience giving a generous license on the side of what is fair and noble. Such, at least, is my experience.

I cannot speak of my work, either in public or private, without giving a word of heartfelt and true gratitude toward their Royal Highnesses the Prince and Princess of Wales for their gracious and continued sympathy and support in it.

At one of the first public recitals I gave in London (June 19, 1883), they were present with a large party and suite. The Prince, I think, did not often go to afternoon functions of this kind, and the favour was, therefore, the more to be appreciated.

It was at the Prince's Hall, Piccadilly. One of the horses in the Princess's carriage was frightened in some way just as they drove up to the hall, and a rather serious accident might have occurred; but the Prince of Wales jumped out, and, with instant presence of mind, seized the head of the horse. It delayed their arrival a little. Her Royal Highness was, as I have always found her, the most attentive and sympathetic of auditors.

But there are days when one seems made of wood. I suppose every executant artist knows the experience. I could not recite that afternoon with any heart or conviction. It was all perfunctory and cold. Occasions of this sort, too, are rather disturbing. As organizer of the entertainment, there was much to see after, and much to tie one's thoughts to the place and the moment; and all this is disastrous to the disengaged mind that is required for any good work.

The Prince of Wales had to leave at the end of the first part. 'I am going on,' he said to me, 'to another kind of recital, where I do not think the speaking will be nearly so good.' It was to the House, to hear a great debate. 'You must put in the story of the *Faithful Soul*,' he said, as he was going away; 'the Princess is so fond of that.'

The Princess of Wales herself kindly stayed until the end, and she gave me very kind and prettily turned thanks as she went away.

I have had the honour, too, of reciting at Sandringham House—Saturday, March 31, 1883. It was to me a very interesting occasion. The party assembled was notable; and, having had the experiences I have received in great country houses on like occasions, I could not but admire the way, at once firm and artistic, yet perfectly gracious, with which the Princess of Wales arranged that the recitations should be properly listened to, and that nothing should distract or deny attention. This courtesy and good taste is, however, a distinguishing mark of our Royal Family. I have heard my father speak of it in his professional career. Nor was this the first occasion by many whereon I had witnessed it, and benefited by it. Only a short time before this recital at Sandringham, I was giving a recital for a charity in a private house, which had been lent for the occasion. The Duchess of Teck was present. She came upstairs whilst I was reciting. I noticed her charming grace and tact. She refused to come into the room whilst I was speaking, and beckoned to the people who were near the door to remain quiet. She stood there till the piece was over, and then came in. Would that ladies, great and little, would follow her example on like occasions! The Duchess of Teck has always been most kind to me. She is a perfect listener, and misses no point.

In one sense only was the evening at Sandringham a disappointment to me. I had hoped to have recited before the Queen. When the date was first fixed it was arranged for one of the nights when the Queen was expected to be staying at Sandringham. The hope of reciting before Her Majesty was peculiarly interesting and pleasant to me, remembering her gracious kindness to my father years ago, and how she sympathized with his work, and accorded it her patronage and favour. I was, therefore, doubly sorry when I heard that the Queen was unfortunately unable to go to Sandringham. The engagement for this recital, however, was to stand good.

I found an interesting house-party assembled. The Duke of Cambridge and the Duchess of Teck, the Archbishop of Canterbury, Mr. and Mrs. Gladstone, and Lord and Lady Roseberry were of the party; Sir Dighton and Lady Probyn, and Lord and Lady Romney were also present. There were about thirty people altogether. I had never recited before the present Primate or the ex-Premier, and their presence made me wish I could choose recitations of a less popular kind than those I had noted down for recitation. I had met Dr. Benson years ago at Eversley Rectory, when he was at Wellington, but that was long before I thought of taking to my present profession. Mr. Gladstone talked to me of my work, and of the recitations I had given. His manner carries with it the pleasant conviction of a personal interest in the subject of which he is speaking. This exercises a great charm, and is potent, because one feels it is real, and not merely assumed out of politeness or kindness. The influence of his appearance and presence is great, and partakes almost of the nature of personal fascination. Mrs. Gladstone was most gracious. She told me that Mr. Gladstone was very pleased. She said it was a great pleasure—she added, an unexpected pleasure—to have such an intellectual evening; which I thought was hard on those assembled.

The Duke of Cambridge, with the strong tender-heartedness of the true soldier, was much moved by a piece I was asked to recite, called *The Newsboy's Debt*—a piece the late Dean of Westminster first told me of. His Royal Highness spoke to me of my father, remembering him well—a remembrance in which the Prince of Wales joined very kindly; and in conclusion he applied the word 'clever' to me, with a cordiality of expression which left no doubt as to his gracious wish to make the words carry all possible conviction and assurance to my mind. I had never had approval that pleased me better. The Archbishop asked after my brother and his wife. But I suspect the pieces I recited were somewhat too popular to appeal very much to his literary way of regarding such work. In private recitals I often feel painfully the impossibility of pleasing all my listeners in the choice of recitations; and of course on that occasion my leading wish was to recite whatever the Princess of Wales wished to hear. I gave

The Legend Beautiful (with music) .. *Longfellow.*
George Lee .. .. *Hamilton Aïdé.*
The Story of the Faithful Soul
  (with music) .. .. .. *Adelaide Anne Procter.*
The Signalman .. .. *C. H.*
The Building of St. Sophia (with music) *Baring Gould.*
The Newsboy's Debt .. .. *Anon.*

I was to have given a humorous recitation I had selected from *Vanity Fair*, but it was twelve o'clock, and the Princess rose.

It is curious how difficult it is to choose recitations at these times; how hedged about one is in a private room in such work. It is all on a totally different platform in public, and the pieces assume a different aspect. The word 'platform' suggests one practical reason of this. The platform itself simplifies matters. It removes the speaker into another world. It justifies and permits a wide appeal. As long as I am on the same level with my listeners, the personal and social considerations dominate the occasion. And thus of every piece it has to be searchingly asked, 'Is there no offence in it?' In public the question is one easy to negative. The field is freer, and admits drama at once more delicate, more strong, and more intimate.

On one occasion when I was going to recite before the Princess of Wales at Lady Probyn's (Park House, Sandringham), I sat down before dinner to make out a programme of the recitations to be given, and began, as is my custom, by putting down all the pieces I could think of as suitable. Thus I made a list of seventy pieces, from which to choose six for that evening. Any half-dozen of them would have formed a good programme for the occasion had the recital been in a public hall. But, on taking each piece and putting it, as it were, into the circumstances of a private drawing-room, and surrounding it with the atmosphere it would have to breathe, I found my list of seventy pieces dwindling down to eleven, as possibly fitted to the time and place: and of this remnant I sorely mistrusted five. It was a case of the old Scotch woman's true Church, which was found to consist of herself and her husband John, and she was 'nae so sure o' John!'

The evening I refer to at Lady Probyn's was one of the most pleasant of many pleasant and interesting evenings spent there. I think it made the eighth time I had the honour of reciting before the Princess of Wales. But I was asked to give some of the pieces I gave the very first time I went to Sandringham— notably Anne Procter's most *Faithful Soul* and Hamilton Aïdé's *George Lee*.

Prince George of Wales asked me to recite Tennyson's *Revenge*. I had recited before the Duke of Clarence a short while before, at Trinity Hall, Cambridge. These evenings at Park House, Sandringham, have been most memorable and delightful episodes in my work.

Perhaps no form of entertainment, or expression of dramatic art, has been so well abused and so mercilessly caricatured, as has Recitation during the last few years. Nor is the reason far to seek. For myself I have hailed the abuse and enjoyed the caricature, as sharp and necessary remedies for a growing danger to an art I love, and which has been sorely injured by a fatal popularity.

A few years ago—when I first began my work—Mr. Brandram was, broadly speaking, alone in the field. Amateur reciting was almost unknown (O happy days!); and even amongst actors and actresses it was a form of art but little used or esteemed. Now all that is altered. The times are changed. The field is crowded in every direction; public reciters are many; the stage has owned its poor relation, and the amateur world has seized on the art with unconscionable rapacity. To me it is surprising that, in face of the very immature and strange exhibitions that have been labelled 'reciting,' both in public and private, the art has survived. It argues the possession of an admirable vigour and vitality. But that it should be by many shunned and looked askance at, is not astonishing. For who has not suffered from its evil and desolating claims for silence and a hearing at 'at homes' and social gatherings? Has not recitation added a new terror to society, and a new danger to domestic furniture? When will the day come when people will realize and believe that recitation is not an easy, but a very difficult art?

That it is truly an art is, I think, clear and provable. Lecky, in his *History of the Rise of*

Rationalism, and speaking of the theatre, says, 'This amusement, which has ever proved one of the chief delights, and one of the most powerful incentives to genius, had at the same time the rare privilege of acting with equal power upon the opposite extremes of intellect, and is even now almost the only work connecting thousands with intellectual pursuits.' There seems no reason why Recitation should not share these honours with the stage, for it is eminently capable of 'acting with equal power on the opposite extremes of intellect.' Longfellow has recorded in a sonnet his delight in the 'Precious evenings! all too swiftly fled!' when he listened to Mrs. Fanny Kemble's readings of Shakespeare's plays. Many are the spoken and written confessions of interest and pleasure in recitation that I could quote. Whilst remembering with lively pleasure the tears and laughter, the awakened sympathy and imagination, of audiences into whose lives, I fear, little of imagination or sympathy entered, I cannot doubt but that recitation can also equally touch with a refreshing and refining hand that class which has little time or power to receive the lessons of the greater parent-arts. Recitation needs a special gift and a special training in the artist. It touches the material employed not only with the bare truth of an interpreting voice, but also with a force and a delicacy that are its own. It is a perfect medium whereby the world may be

> '. . . wrought
> To sympathy with hopes and fears it heeded not.'

It is singularly complete and self-contained. It encloses the old primitive way of telling stories in verse by rhythmic repetition, and also the more modern and civilized presentation of drama by the actor. It has been steadily growing in artistic development and in public favour for many years. If true to itself, and if its position be not undermined by the incapacity of well-meaning but imperfect aspirants, it may well look forward to association and brotherhood with those older executive arts by which literature and music are brought home to the ears and to the hearts of a world that is ready and willing to listen if only the right voice will speak.

II.
S OF REMINISCENCE.

'And live again in memory.'
TENNYSON.

II.

My father, artist and manager—Balfe—Mrs. W. Clifford—
My mother—A feat of memory—Macready—Un-
realized ideals—On the stage—At Sheffield—Eversley
—Charles Kingsley—Robert Browning—Ruskin—
Hamilton Aïdé—Frederick Locker—Lord Tennyson—
Mrs. Fanny Kemble—George Eliot—Dean Stanley—
The Emperor Frederick—Dr. Vaughan—Dr. John
Brown—Sir Henry Taylor—Augustus Hare—Mrs.
Procter—Madame Mohl—Lady Pollock—Delaunay—
Lord Houghton—Lady Martin—Lady Freake—The
Waverley tableaux—The capital M.

My father was of a north-country family. On his mother's side he was of Scotch descent. He was a very handsome man, of a fine presence and dignified bearing : and he possessed great physical strength. It was a curious fate which linked his fortunes with art and the operatic stage—one, I fancy, that he would scarcely have chosen for himself ; for he was a born lover of the country, and his tastes were those which led to open air and country life.

He had, however, a very true love for his

art: for he was not only gifted with a beautiful voice, but also with a distinct and discriminating love of music. He was very fond of acting, and had great dramatic talent. I own that I am glad to remember that he 'created' the tenor parts in the only two English operas of his day that seem likely to live, namely, *The Bohemian Girl*, by Balfe, and *Maritana*, by Wallace. They have secured their place. And it is, I think, no exaggeration to say that the enormous success my father made in the parts of Thaddeus and Don Cæsar de Bazan was distinctly instrumental in securing to these works in the first place public attention, and in keeping them high in public favour. There were many representatives of the soprano *rôles* in these operas, but during my father's lifetime there was, in effect, but one Thaddeus and one Don Cæsar. In the first success of *The Bohemian Girl*, the sale of the ballad *When other Lips*—or, as it is also called, *Then You'll remember Me*—was something prodigious and unprecedented.* The originality and beauty of the melody was, of course, the real root of the success; but in the case of every such

---

* Over 80,000 copies of the song were sold in the first year of its production.

long it must be admitted that at the starting-point the singer who sings the song affects its fortune, and opens the first flood of popularity.

I have often heard my father speak of his mingled pleasure and embarrassment when, at one of the Ancient Concerts, he was personally addressed by the Duke of Wellington, who was sitting in the front row of the audience. At the end of the song the Great Duke rose and called out, 'Mr. Harrison! Mr. Harrison! I wish to tell you that I saw you a few nights ago in the *Beggar's Opera*, and that I was delighted with your admirable performance. I wish to express publicly to you my pleasure, and my good wishes for your success.'

Doubtless, too, my father's admirable acting did much to build up his success. Strange to say, I never saw *The Bohemian Girl*. But I can recall his performance of Don Cæsar de Bazan in *Maritana*, and it certainly was a fine piece of acting. In his hands it possessed a high tone, a certain gallantry and chivalry of bearing through all the degradation and dare-devilry of the character. Even in the rags and drunkenness of the first act he made the man a very fine gentleman.

The same power of delineation and of high bearing was observable in many of his performances. In the *Puritan's Daughter*, an opera by Balfe, he played Rochester. Here again his courtliness and gallantry of manner was apparent, even under the very questionable circumstances in which the librettist places the Merry Monarch and his boon companion. These parts—Rochester and Don Cæsar— might soon sink to vulgarity and coarseness if not acted with a nice sense of touch, and remembrance of who the men are. With my father they were fine bits of comedy. Something of the same art made his performance of Manuel, the supposed muleteer in the *Rose of Castile*, interesting; for the discovery of the true position of the character at the end of the opera was hinted at under the muleteer-disguise all through the story. In the *Crown Diamonds*, in Macfarren's *She Stoops to Conquer*, and in an opera by Wallace called *Love's Triumph* (which, by the way, possessed the charm of a really admirable and witty libretto by Planché), the distinction of his acting was something I have never seen equalled on the later lyric stage.

A part which greatly exercised his mind was Corentin in *Dinorah*. He was physically unsuited to it, and he felt that the ridiculous timidity of the character would seem almost grotesque in him. But he redeemed the personal cowardice of the Breton peasant by a courage born of avarice, and thus brought the part within the scope of his pourtrayal. It was no small compliment to the performance of this opera altogether, under his and Miss Louisa Pyne's joint management, that the Queen and the Prince Consort came to hear it three times in the course of a fortnight. Miss Pyne was the Dinorah, my father Corentin, and Santley (his first appearance, I believe) the Hoel. The band, the chorus, and the mounting of the opera, were the same as at the Italian Opera.

In later years fate seemed against the undertaking. The first serious blow was the death of the Prince Consort. He was greatly interested in the work. I believe I am speaking accurately when I say that there had been some assurance given that if the undertaking made itself good for three years, influence would be exerted to bring forward the consideration of a subsidy from the state for national opera.* It was in this third year that the Prince Consort died. The theatre was closed for a short time, I believe; and when it was reopened the royal box was closed by command, the curtains being drawn and draped with crape. But, of course, the general mourning, and this particular sign of it in the theatre, kept the house nearly empty. From fine receipts the business fell down to a figure that meant nightly loss. Indeed, I think it is true to say, broadly speaking, that success never visited the undertaking again. Each subsequent season represented another deep step towards ruin.

Once they had *Faust* in rehearsal. This was before it was produced in England. My father was very anxious to produce it. But, strange to say, he and Miss Pyne were urgently advised not to do so by Balfe and by Alfred Mellon. Such advice seems inexplicable. But I distinctly remember hearing my father remind Balfe of the circumstance years afterwards, when the success of *Faust* was assured and Balfe himself was raving about the beauty

* 'The prince had informed Louisa Pyne that if the performances could be continued a certain time, influence should be used to bring the matter before Parliament.'— *The Light of Other Days*, Willert Beale.

of the music. We were staying with Balfe at the time, at his place in Hertfordshire. It was the year before my father died.

Another curious check, as it seems, was given in the matter of *Tannhäuser*. The production of this opera was under discussion for some time. We used to talk a good deal about it, I remember, and my mother and I worked hard at the pianoforte score. My father went to Paris to meet Wagner, and I find in an old note-book of his a brief entry just recording the fact that a meeting had taken place; and that Wagner was 'very pleasant, and said very complimentary things about our work at Covent Garden.' Also that he was 'a particularly impressive man both in manner and in appearance.' 'A strong-minded man,' he writes, 'original in thought, and wonderfully decisive. He is very pleased at being honoured by the Emperor of the French wishing the *Tannhäuser* here in December. I settled all with him for the production of that opera in February, and when we parted he expressed himself as being very pleased.' I find, however, no further record, and it is certain that the opera was not produced at the time named. I take it that the venture was too great. Wagner's work was practically unknown in England then; and the notion that it was 'the music of the future,' was based, I fear, less on prophetic certainty than on a doubt of its ever having a present.

It is, however, curious and sad to me to know that my father wished to produce these two great representative operas, and even entered into business preliminaries about them, and that in both instances the intentions and wishes were unfulfilled.

Faust was indeed performed under his exclusive management at Her Majesty's Theatre, but that was some years after it had been produced at the Italian Opera. On that occasion Mr. Sims Reeves was the *Faust*, Mr. Santley the *Valentine*, and Miss Louisa Pyne the *Marguerite*. Signor Arditi conducted.

Mr. Willert Beale, in his reminiscences, *The Light of Other Days*, says—

'No two singers are more closely identified with the progress of English dramatic music than are Louisa Pyne and William Harrison. Through their exertions English opera, when it seemed doomed to perish from neglect, was made to flourish. They gave English composers liberal commissions, and produced their works with the greatest care.* It is no exaggeration to say that Harrison is associated with more success on the English stage than any other tenor singer of the present half-century. He was the original Thaddeus in the *Bohemian Girl*, and well I recollect, although a mere boy at the time, the prodigious uproar occasioned by his singing "Then you'll remember me," on the first night the opera was produced. The majority of the audience insisted on hearing the song a second time. To this there were numerous opponents, and the noise made by the rival factions was deafening. Balfe laid down the baton and folded his arms; . . . some minutes elapsed, after which the dissentients gave way, and the song, destined to become a national melody, was sung again. . . . As a manager, Harrison proved himself an able man of business, free from caprice of any kind, strictly impartial, and honourable in all his dealings. He shared the success of Balfe and Wallace in all their principal operas, and has every right to be considered the dramatic tenor *par excellence* of their period.'

* Upwards of two hundred thousand pounds were spent on musical copyrights, libretti, and salaries alone—to say nothing of current expenses of the theatre, scenery, etc., etc.

I suppose it is true to say that nearly every opera that Balfe wrote, and which was produced in England—with the exception of the *Talisman*—was written with the express intention that my father should be the tenor. Six or seven operas of his, I think, were actually produced at Covent Garden. The earlier works, which were the more successful, were written when my father was merely an engaged artist.

It seems strange to us that an opera should be built up on the old lines, and that certain conventional points should be made the centres of success to be worked for. But there is no doubt that it was so with Balfe's operas. One of these points was a ballad for the tenor, generally placed in the third act. Balfe's enthusiasm and energy to achieve this point of success, and his patience in the achievement, were, I have heard my mother say, extraordinary and admirable. He would write tune after tune, and submit them, one by one, to my father for judgment. For he worked with and for his artists. He was never satisfied until he got a melody which was absolutely and unhesitatingly pronounced 'a hit—a palpable hit.' 'Will it do? Say yes or no, without hesitation. We must have it right. I'll go on till it is right. Never mind me. Say yes or no,' he used to say.

He wrote six or seven settings of the words before he hit on the celebrated 'When other lips.' I speak only for verbal remembrance in all this—remembrance of what I have heard my father and mother say. But I believe the following story is true.

Balfe had tried and tried again for the 'right' melody. My father was still dissatisfied, and Balfe was still on the quest. Late one night—or rather in the small hours of the morning—a cab drove up to my father's door, and a mighty peal of the bell startled the household. My father, recognizing Balfe's voice outside, went down and opened the door. Balfe rushed in, waving a roll of music over his head, and calling out, 'I've got it! I've got! I've got it!' He ran upstairs to the drawing-room, sat down at the piano, and awoke the surprised echoes of the night with the now-renowned melody.

Even in my own remembrance I can somewhat parallel the story. For when we were living at St. John's Wood, and the opera of *The Puritan's Daughter* was being composed, I can recollect Balfe driving up early one morning, and shouting to my father as he hurried down the steps that led into the garden, that he had 'got it at last!' The 'it' in this case was a drinking-song which Rochester sings in the second act of the opera. Balfe had tried his hand on it already several times without satisfying himself, or my father.

Listening to the easy and flowing tunes of his operas, one might be tempted to suppose the work they represent must have been somewhat easy and flowing too. But at times it certainly was not, from what I have heard. Like all good work, it meant hard work.

I went with my father once on a visit to Balfe at his place in Hertfordshire (1867, I think it must have been). He was very bright and amusing, and Madame Balfe was an excellent hostess. I remember that I was very much struck by the clever manner in which she had fitted herself into country life. There was a farm attached to the estate, and the property was altogether of some extent. She managed it all. I recollect the bailiff telling my father that she was as good a farmer as any one he had ever known. She positively made it pay!—a circumstance which the bailiff

truly seemed to think little short of the
miraculous. She rose quite early, interviewed
the bailiff and servants, and got through all
the business of the day before the ten-o'clock
breakfast. She dressed quite in country fashion,
and altogether accepted the position with
admirable cleverness and tact; and admirable
perception of its humour also.

Balfe was a short man, unimpressive in
appearance, but possessing a great geniality of
manner, and a knowledge of the world and all
phases of society. He had a bright Irish wit,
and seemed to have taken life so easily that the
chief expression of his face was one of good
humour. He was full of anecdote and personal
reminiscences, and his stories were often pointed
with a distinct Irish brogue, which gave them
additional zest.

He played a good deal of the music for the
Talisman, which he was then composing; and
he also played and sang to me a setting of some
verses of mine. The music was charming. I
remember, too, that I played sonatas of Beethoven to him all one evening after dinner.
His enthusiasm for the great master was something delightful to witness. His excitement over
the music, indeed, became so great that he sat

down then and there, and showed us how often in his operas he had borrowed a *motif* or passage from the *Sonatas* and *Symphonies*. He owned to it in the most naïve and candid way. 'Ye can't do better,' he said, with a beaming face, 'than go to the fountain-head, and come away with a cupful! There are two composers I've never scrupled to borrow from —one's Beethoven, the other's meself!'"

My mother's maiden name was Ellen Clifford. She was the daughter of Mrs. W. Clifford, who was well known in theatrical circles fifty years ago. Mrs. Clifford was the daughter of a leading physician in Bath, a man of means and standing, in the days when Bath was a centre of life and fashion. Her mother was a famous beauty—a fact which an old miniature in my possession still testifies. My grandmother, Mrs. W. Clifford, married, when she was only seventeen years of age, Mr. W. Clifford, a subaltern in the 30th Regiment. It was a runaway match, probably foolish and ill-considered; but, at any rate, it was a true love-affair. Both families, however, not unnaturally, hotly resented it. The young couple were excommunicated with what seems to have been unnecessary harshness, and found themselves

ependent on the pay of a young officer of
expensive tastes and extravagant habits.

I have always fancied that he was a sort of
George Osborn. The only picture I have of
him is a rough pencil drawing, made by a
brother officer the night before the regiment
started for the Peninsula. My mother used to
tell me that it was a sketch made, half in fun,
after dinner. 'See, Mrs. Clifford, I will make
a sketch of your husband, and give it to you as
a pledge I'll take care of him.' I have the drawing now, the pencilling still quite dark and
unblurred, the paper yellow and frail with
age.

He was wounded in one of the many smaller
engagements of the campaign, and returned
to England only to die on landing (1814). The
young widow, in impetuous faithfulness to him,
refused to be reconciled with his family; and,
being left in something like poverty, with
two little girls (of whom my mother was the
younger), went on the stage. In those days
it was almost the only avenue of work open to
a lady. It was uphill work for her—young,
attractive, and without influence. Under some
circumstances it seemed probable that she
might have risen to eminence as an actress.

As it was, she made her name well known and respected.

From the few people I have met who remember her, I hear she was a most charming woman—vivacious, clever, and possessing a fine strength of character. My mother adored her; and, although Mrs. Clifford died soon after I was born, it is difficult for me to believe that I do not remember her—so living a presence and influence was her memory in our home. Truly as she lives in my name, she also lives deeply in my reverence.

There is good evidence that her capability as an actress was of no mean order. She acted with Edmund Kean, with Mrs. Siddons, with the Kembles, and with Macready; and in later years she was a member of the Haymarket Theatre, in the days of the elder Farren and of Mrs. Glover. She was in the original cast of *The Lady of Lyons*, in which play, Lady Martin has told me, she was really admirable: raising the small part she was assigned (Madame Deschapelles) to distinction by the excellence of her acting. John Kemble said she was the finest Lady Macbeth, 'after Sarah Siddons,' that he had ever seen. And Sir Walter Scott, who was present once in the

Edinburgh Theatre when she was acting in *Guy Mannering*, was so excited and pleased with her performance that he exclaimed, 'Whilst that woman lives Meg Merrilies will never die!'

My mother was on the stage for a short time before her marriage. She made her appearance on the stage, I think, at the Exeter Theatre, when it stood high amongst provincial theatres. At a party I went to one night in the May of 1880 I met an old gentleman—a great playgoer—who told me that he recollected seeing my mother make her first appearance in the part of Perdita. He said it was a most graceful and charming performance. Many playgoers of his day, he said, greatly regretted her retirement from the stage when she married.

In *Records of My Girlhood*, Mrs. Fanny Kemble mentions a wonderful feat of memory which my mother performed. It happened thus. My grandmother, Mrs. W. Clifford, used to suffer with headaches so terrible that they quite prostrated her. She had one of these cruel visitations one day when she was acting Goneril with Macready in *King Lear*. My mother, then quite a girl, went to the theatre to explain to Mr. Macready that it was impossible for

Mrs. Clifford to act that night. 'She cannot play the part?' he said. 'What is to be done? My dear, you must.' She protested, appealed, even with tears; but he spoke most kindly, encouraged and persuaded her, and at last she consented to do it. She went home, and, with simulated cheerfulness, told her mother what she had consented to do. Mrs. Clifford instantly started up, declaring it was impossible; that she would not permit her child to play so painful a part, etc., etc. However, she finally gave way before entreaties lovingly given, and the mastering influence of the headache.

It was then nearly two o'clock. My mother shut herself in her room, and began the tremendous task of learning the part. It is a long one, and difficult to study. In the stage phraseology of those days, it was some fourteen 'lengths.' She played it at night letter-perfect. Macready said it was one of the most remarkable efforts of memory he had ever known.

During her short career on the stage my mother acted a good deal with Macready. She had the greatest admiration for his art. But he was a singularly agitating actor to act with. He had, it seems, a way of pausing in the middle of his speeches, and glaring at you in a questioning way, as if he expected you to speak. On one of these occasions he paused so long, and looked so increasingly surprised and angry, that my mother actually began her next speech, without waiting for the cue; whereupon he gripped her arm hard, and muttered in his usual fashion, 'Er! er! er! Keep quiet!' continuing to glare in questioning silence. At last he took up his speech again, and gave the cue. 'Why did you begin to speak without your cue?' he asked, when they came off. She murmured something about the pause being so natural that it deceived even her, and the pretty flattery mollified the great man.

At rehearsal he was, as most great actors are, a tyrant. In some piece, when she had to fall into his arms (*Coriolanus*, I think), he required the action to be done in some peculiar way, and it had to be repeated so often and emphatically, that a certain pretty new bonnet was sadly disorganized. But the next day a more glorified bit of millinery arrived, with a note wishing her acceptance of it in lieu of the damaged head-gear.

In *William Tell* (Sheridan Knowles) he produced a great effect by rushing off the stage in one of the scenes, shouting, 'Gesler!

Gesler!' This shout was heard dying far away into the distance. To gain this effect, he used to rush about the back of the stage, behind the scenes, down a long passage, and into his dressing-room, not ceasing to shout till the dressing-room door was shut. The place was kept clear, and woe betide any ill-starred mortal who met him 'in his wild career.'

At the Norwich Theatre one night, in *Virginius* (Sheridan Knowles), he so throttled and maltreated his Marcus (?), that the gentleman who played that part—a Mr. John Smith, the manager's son—determined to prepare himself on future occasions for the rough usage he was to receive. So, having more regard for personal comfort than histrionic effect, and secure in his position as the manager's son, he appeared in the throttling scene with a great wad of cotton-wool and towelling round his neck, under the toga, infinitely to Macready's dismay and measureless indignation.

Once, on the occasion of casting a new play a very insignificant part was assigned to a man who held a rather high position in public estimation, as well as in his own. He was sorely offended, and thought it would be detrimental to his reputation. Angry, hurt and yet somewhat frightened, he went up to Macready and said, 'Mr. Macready, sir! this is too bad. I must say I feel deeply hurt. Sir! I have *only one line* to say in this play!' Macready gave his usual little exclamatory grunt, 'Er! er! well. Mind you say it well!' and passed on.

On the night when my father appeared in London, one of the first persons to congratulate him and my mother on the success achieved was Mr. Macready.

It is not surprising that, in spite of loving persuasions, and a home influence curiously far removed from the theatre, I determined early in life to go on the stage. But my ideal at that time had somewhat of the vaulting ambition that o'erleaps itself. I cannot accuse myself of not aiming high enough. Long before I left school I had determined to be a poet, a dramatist, a painter, and an actor—all together! It was a beautiful ideal; but it was not to be realized. I, however, did my best at the time. I wrote heaps of verses—poor things, and not always mine own either! One long poem I remember I sent to Moxon, the publisher, and positively got a note in return that was encouraging, though the MS. was *not* accepted.

I painted a wonderful oil picture: 'This is the forest primæval, the murmuring pines and the hemlocks;' and another still more wonderful, 'Nigh unto Trophonius;' and another most wonderful of all, 'In the lonely Thebaid.' Then I enacted, on school Speech-day, 'Cardinal Wolsey,' in the great scene from Henry VIII. And I wrote plays. The most ambitious of these was founded on Alfred de Vigny's novel of *Cinq Mars*. It had many names, being called in turn, *M. le Grand*, *Ambition*, *The Conspirator*, *The Shadow of the Church*, *Fortune's Fool*, and *The Cardinal's Puppet*. I think the last name was best by far! It was in five acts, and was written in blank verse. Not a line of it remains, as far as I know. And yet, perhaps, it has not disappeared as entirely as that. For in it there was a part written for my father. His voice was failing him at the time, and he thought of taking to acting. In this part I introduced two songs. He sent them to Balfe, and it is certain that he set them; for, as I have already stated, I went with my father to visit him at his place in Hertfordshire (Rowney Abbey), and whilst we were there Balfe played the songs to us. One was uncommonly pretty and taking. It was a legend, with a refrain and a chorus. Balfe himself was pleased with the song. I have not an idea what became of it; and when I saw Madame Balfe in late years, I quite forgot to ask her about it. It would scarcely have been destroyed.

Of a very different calibre was another dramatic work I perpetrated. It was a comedy in the Robertsonian style—yclept *Sunshine and Shadow*, or some such title. I had seen *Ours*, and *Caste*, and *Play*, and was fired with enthusiasm for the new style of comedy, and with personal hero-worship for Mr. and Mrs. Bancroft. I suppose there was some sort of form in the piece I wrote, for my father, to encourage me doubtless, positively wrote to Mr. Bancroft about it. An appointment was made, and I went to read my comedy to my realized ideals. They were very kind. What must they have thought of it? I wonder if they have forgotten all about the episode? It was far too pleasurable for me to forget. I recollect that Mr. Bancroft talked the MS. over with me, showed me some of the faults of construction, and the lack of contrast in the characters. I don't think he found any fault with the dialogue. I don't think there was anything, in one sense, to find fault with! As far as I remember, it was singularly blameless.

I never see Mr. and Mrs. Bancroft without thinking of that comedy, and remembering how kindly she laughed distinctly three times. I don't wonder. I thought it very kind then that she should laugh at all. I think it kinder now that she did not laugh permanently.

I carried out one of my intentions, however; I went upon the stage. I appeared at the Theatre Royal, Manchester, as Corporal Nym in *The Merry Wives of Windsor*. Any one more tragically unfitted for the part, both mentally and physically, even a stage manager in his most inspired moments could not hope to select. It was a cruel and a crushing blow to one of my Ideals. Indeed, I don't think I have ever recovered the entire ideality of the subject since that very harsh realization.

I once fulfilled a six months' engagement—from the new year to the midsummer—at the Theatre Royal, Sheffield (1869). It was shortly after my father's death, and I was between eighteen and nineteen.

On the whole I have pleasant recollections of my time at Sheffield, although the life had aspects that were strange, and not always exhilarating. Every one in the theatre was very kind to me.

I have studied and played as many as ten and twelve parts a week. I will not say that anything but the 'cues' were given *verbatim*; and these were doubtless often arrived at by short cuts as startling and prompt as that of the nervous actor who, on the speech of the Doge in the trial scene from the *Merchant of Venice*, cut down the whole of the lengthy speech into the first and last lines, and paralyzed the stage by saying—

'Shylock, the world thinks, and I think so too . . .
—We all expect a gentle answer, Jew!'

I used to take my part in melodrama, comedy, tragedy, and farce. It was good practice in a way, but all too rough and haphazard. Its chief practical utility should have been to cure me of shyness. But I do not think it succeeded in this ; perhaps it even added to it.

I always had—on the stage, and possibly off it too—far too much of that forgotten virtue, or vice, as the opinion of it may be, that same shyness. The word can be found in any old dictionary. It is a quality that has no virtue in it on the stage, whatever it may possess in private life. It is about as desirable for a Zermatt guide to be subject to vertigo, as for an actor to be shy. When I say shy, I do not mean anything to do with nervousness. That is an entirely different quality, and is, I believe, as necessary to the actor as shyness is fatal. I never met a good actor who was not nervous; but, also, I never met one who was shy. I hope, however, that I have sufficient assurance (at least apparently) on the platform not to fear owing to having had none on the boards. Yet I recollect that even then the incapacitating self-consciousness left me when I was alone on the stage.

At this theatre I attempted my first public recitation. Our 'leading lady,' Mrs. Eburne, was organizing a benefit, and I asked her to let me give a recitation between the pieces. She was always very kind to me, and she consented. I saw my name announced to recite *Locksley Hall*. It seems to me that it was a curious departure for a shy young man. I believe all my comrades were astounded at my impudence. Many of them told me they would not face such an ordeal for that Alexander-like bribe that is vaguely summed up as 'worlds.' To go on and recite a long poem seemed to them the height of assurance. But I did not view it so, and shyness departed from

ne on that occasion. I ought to have taken
he hint at once, and adopted this form of
lramatic expression as the one suited to me.
I really think I have reason to be proud of the
eat of reciting *Locksley Hall* that night. To
1old a Sheffield audience in those days, quiet
ind attentive, to a long and introspective poem,
between the excitement of a melodrama and
:he laughter of a farce, was no slight or easy
:ask. But I undertook it with all the insolence
of youth and inexperience. And insolence was
rewarded—as it often is, at Sheffield and else-
where. I had a recall. The stage doorkeeper
was a great friend of mine. He had, I know,
the very lowest opinion of me as an actor,
but he liked me as a friend. He came to the
'wings' to hear *Locksley Hall*, with what expectations I know not, but his face looked prepared for the worst. He was almost too
astonished to speak. But at last he said,
'Well, I *am* surprised! You did it well. No
error. My! you let 'em have it! I shouldn't
have thought you'd have had the cheek.'

It is a delightful thing to have positively
played in *The Orange Girl*, and dramas of that
kind; to have been both Riber and Golotz in
The Miller and his Men:

Riber. Curse on this chance ! We have lost him !
Golotz. No matter. A time may come.
Riber. A time *shall* come, and quickly, too !

[*Exeunt* L. V. E.

To have portrayed—and what a portrayal it must have been!—a pirate waving the *Jolly Roger* in one hand, and pointing a pistol in the other; to have moved in scenes that were literally described in the bill as *On Board the Lugger*, *Above the Powder Magazine*, and *In the Depths of the Forest*. I am glad to have appeared as Count Wintersen in *The Stranger*, and as Catesby in *Guy Fawkes*. In the latter part, by the way, I was so eager to be shot that I fell headlong backwards before the volley was fired. I have a charming memory, too, of an episode in some modern drama of the melodramatic and sensational kind. I was the villain, and had to appear casually at a first-floor window in evening dress and with a cigarette, and hold a colloquy with a low accomplice in crime who was concealed beneath the window in a lime-lit garden. At this window I appeared with seeming easy grace, but in reality with dizzy anguish; for to get up to it I had to mount a tall rickety ladder, which was held up by two men at the ngle necessary for me to appear at the opening without leaning against the flimsy scene. I mounted the ladder and assumed what appearance of ease I could, pretending to lean out of the window. But, according as the men got tired or renewed their strength, I was depressed until I nearly sank out of sight, or was elevated to dangerous height. At one time I remember clinging to an almost perpendicular ladder, as a drowning man to a straw; and, on remonstrating in a loud undertone, I was lowered so quickly as to precipitate me forward with Punch-like energy. It was a terrible scene. I was told it had been known to go better. I have played Melter Moss in the *Ticket of Leave Man* one night, and County Paris in *Romeo and Juliet* the next. And — crown and triumph of memorable parts!—I have played George Barnwell, and addressed the audience as 'Be warned, ye youths, who see my sad despair.'

My rooms were a great centre of interest to me during this sojourn at Sheffield. They were much decorated with drawings, fencing-foils, and various schoolboy treasures. My landlady, Mrs. Nutt—a woman in a thousand! —was devoted to me, and made me very comfortable. She took an almost measureless pride in my rooms, and, I was told, exhibited them to admiring neighbours and friends when I was out. And, if I seemed low-spirited, she would point majestically to the walls and say, 'Look round you, sir, and see how elegant and home-like it is!'

Mr. Nutt was a rather feckless person, I think. He was seldom seen, but on occasions he was distinctly heard. He went away for a long time to some neighbouring factory place. After his return I asked about him, and hoped he was well. 'Yes, thank you, sir,' said his wife; 'but you know, sir, how true the old verse is, that "Satan finds some mischief still for idle hands to do;" and Nutt is out of work just at present.'

Mrs. Nutt was very good to me. The wisdom of the serpent was occasionally employed by her to carry out her designs of kindness and care towards me. An anonymous hamper of good things arrived one day. It appeared to be duly directed to me, and I was told that it had arrived by 'a sort of railway van' during my absence at rehearsal. But I found that there were no official marks or stamps on it, save one which was two years ld; and that the reverse of the card sewn on the hamper with my name and address, showed it to be one of Mrs. Nutt's cards bearing the legend 'Furnished Apartments.'

Opposite the house there was a big forge. I used to see the glare of the furnaces, and hear mysterious and woful noises—thumps and bangs, and a curious wheezing and coughing, as of iron and steel lungs that were slightly congested. Most of the days in the winter, and in what is loosely called the spring, were dark with an Egyptian darkness wrought by the black smokes of innumerable factory chimneys. Sheffield, to a fanciful and uncommercial mind, looks like a sort of mild Inferno at times. The reek of smoke and the roar of fire get on one's nerves. The light of the forge-flame opposite was often so fierce that it conquered the half-hearted dusk which Sheffield is humorous enough to call daylight, and lit up my little den, stencilling the window in angry red across the ceiling and opposite wall. Whereupon I would hum the chorus of demons from *Robert Diable*, and feel sufficiently depressed. But there were not many days when I was at home to watch these lurid exhibitions. Rehearsals from ten till two were an almost daily business.

Then parts had to be written out, and committed to the troubled waters of memory, and dresses for the part or parts of that night had to be selected and arranged.

Sometimes, if I were free and the day were bright—such combination of liberty and light was naturally rare—I would get a long walk on to the hills overlooking the town. The country around Sheffield has been lovely. There are beautiful bits still to be found, and to me there has always been a strange and weird attraction in the factory country. It has a wild, ruined beauty, of its own, an ugly picturesqueness which is curiously moving. Even where the country is flattest and tamest, and the defeat and degradation of natural beauty the most complete, there is still a sort of dark fascination about the region. The pathos is often intense, even tragic. The person must be a sentimentalist, I think, who does not see the wonderful drama of our great 'Black Country,' and of the flaming cities of forge and foundry. A great artist would, I am persuaded, find subjects there that would be magnificent. I often have wondered why, in these days when the world is a bit weary of mere prettiness, and finds its lines of beauty falling often

A TRANSITION.   127

in such unpromising places, painters of the modern school have not sought this extraordinarily picturesque country, with its splendid effects of light and shade, and its constant suggestion of drama.

I believe that the season during which I was at the Sheffield Theatre was the last year of its having a regular 'stock company.' The system has almost, if not entirely, passed away now. I am glad to have had the experience. I stayed on some time after the regular season, as two or three 'star' companies were due, and in some of the pieces to be given there were a few parts to be filled in with local talent. So I saw the dreary winter change into spring and summer. I remember bright days and lovely evenings when I wandered far and wide into the beautiful Yorkshire and Derbyshire country. At the middle of June the engagement terminated, and I went to Eversley. I remember the last night at the theatre, and the dressing-room at the top of the theatre, looking strange and bright with the glory of the midsummer sunset. The next evening I was watching the sunset from the garden of my brother's cottage at Eversley.

At Eversley that summer I decided to quit the stage and go to college.

Autobiography, however, does not, in any set form, enter into the scheme of this volume any more than it finds a place in the note-books from whence the volume is built up. In them I merely find reminiscences scattered about as circumstances or places suggested. I endeavour to put some sort of sequence into these reminiscences in these pages. But often I fear there is no sequence possible, and then I must trust that the pages may perhaps find it in the interest of 'the gentle reader.'

The reminiscences of my own life and the lives of those dear to me were generally started by places. Thus a visit to Sheffield (to give a recital there) suggested the last few pages anent my theatrical experiences; and in another note-book I find that a visit to Eversley carries on some sort of continuation of the time, and raises the memory of a great man whose influence on my life was marked, and for whom I had the deepest love and reverence—Charles Kingsley. I quote the passage from my note-book, written at Eversley. It bears the date of June, 1886.

. . . . It is strange and pathetic to me to be here. The place has seen many changes in the last ten years. Externally perhaps there are not many signs of change. Yet even thus, I think, change is more marked than might be expected in a country-side where the nearest railway-station is a question of miles. Eversley is a great fir-tree country, and fir trees grow apace. Roads that used to lead across bits of tufted common and furzy croft are now hedged with tall trees. Points of views are shut out, familiar waysides altered. A greater number of the larger houses round about have changed hands than is usual in such a country, and the new-comers alter the look of the old places. The village itself is perhaps the least changed thing in the neighbourhood. " The Street" and "the Cross" remain much as I remember them in old days. But the subtle difference which is not exactly change makes itself felt everywhere. It has written itself, I think, into the very atmosphere, and it is borne in upon my mind that Eversley is much altered.

I suppose I shall never forget the summer evening when I came to Eversley from Sheffield. Some events are golden milestones in life. That was one to me. I had been six months in Sheffield, acting at the Theatre Royal. What contrast the life, the atmosphere, the surroundings presented! Externally there was nothing in common between the scene I had left and that to which I came—between the *entourage* of the 'second Walking Gentleman' of T. R. Sheffield and of the brother of the curate at Eversley. Small wonder if I was minded sometimes—conscious of sympathies with both—to talk of parochial matters and country life at Sheffield, and of the stage door and the footlights at Eversley.

My brother's cottage at Eversley then was really beautiful, an ideal little country nest. And what a delight, after the gloom and dirt of the northern steel metropolis, to be in the radiant clean summer air and light, with all the lovely and gracious sounds and sights of the country round me!

But the centre of interest at Eversley was the Rectory. Charles Kingsley had been one of my boyhood's heroes. His poetry was to me a very deep and moving music. His *Andromeda* and the ballads were as companions. *Westward Ho!* used to be called 'Clifford's Text-Book' by my father. I knew some of its descriptive pages by heart. Eversley Village Sermons were well-known and well-loved in our home *The Water Babies* had touched running water and flowing tide with Fairyland for us all.

There was something I had fallen in love with in Kingsley's writing. Its beauty enthralled and yet braced me. It was as the stimulating beauty of the seashore or of a noble landscape seen from 'the edge of some sheep-trimmed down' on a summer day. It had the sensuousness of a beauty which bewitched me; and yet there was a note in it that stirred a subtle home-sickness for a beauty greater and higher than eye could see or ear could hear. Thus it was no mere appeal to the intellect and the ear—great as that may often be—but rather a something hard to describe or give a name to, which made one dimly perceive that there was indeed in

> 'Life, death, and that vast for ever,
> One grand sweet song.'

But of the fulness of the heart the mouth must speak. I should be thankless to the influence that so greatly moved me at that time of my life were I not to speak, without stint of love and praise, of the man who wrought that influence.

It may be imagined, then, with what feelings I looked forward to meeting him, and finding myself face to face with Charles Kingsley.

That face became to me one I looked at with personal affection, as well as with the admiration that I brought with me to the meeting, for familiarity and knowledge but deepened that admiration.

He was one of those very rare examples of an author greater and better even than his work. The world knows well that such examples are but exceptions to the rule in this matter. An author gives you his best in his pages. To know the man is often a slight disillusioning. But it is almost true to say that those who did not know Mr. Kingsley have never read his most beautiful poem or highest sermon; and further, that, once having known him, his own personality and life—for nobility, high tone, wit, humour, and pathos—illuminate his pages so clearly, and stamp them with such individuality, that it is difficult to judge them afterwards impartially, or to see them with eyes of purely impersonal criticism.

All that happy summer—and it was a generous summer of heat and light and song such as he loved—I remained at Eversley. My mother was there too, and my brother Frank. I was at the rectory constantly. Life there was the most perfect thing in its way I have ever seen. The lovely place was a fi shrine for the life within. There was a toucl of romance about it. It raised an enthusiasm in one. And enthusiasm seemed permissible, seemed even natural. To simply admire it would have been unimaginative and silly—like calling a beautiful picture or piece of music 'nice.' One is not likely to see such elements of life and thought combined again. And were lesser folk to attempt the combination the result would probably be confusion and a sense of incongruity. But the large and varied aspects of life brought together in that household were welded together, and became harmonious, from the fact that at their base were two great foundations which never failed—perfect faith and perfect manners.

I do not myself find any incongruity in putting these two things together. For perfect manners, I take it, are something far deeper than any lacquer of courtliness or surface-texture of refinement, and cannot be found save in natures that have an unmovable groundwork of faith of some kind, and a life that is always true to itself.

Also to every one who loved Mr. Kingsley it is pleasant to emphasize this fact of manners. For there was during his lifetime, and is still amongst some of his admirers, a notion that

Kingsley was rather a free-and-easy sort of man—a 'good fellow,' somewhat on the Tom Thurnall and Amyas Leigh lines; a man of undetermined and robust religious opinions, and also of scanty consideration and respect for the social aspects and conditions of life. No greater mistake about him could be made. In both points—at least for himself and in his own attitude of mind and conduct—I should apply no less strong words than rigorous and exact to him. He has recorded, not once or twice, but many times, his intense dislike of the term 'muscular Christian.' His repudiation of it was as complete as his exposure of its dangerous fallacy. True, his sympathies were wide and deep, and his acceptances of life and thought generous and ungrudging. Politically, he could understand the position of Alton Locke, the Chartist; religiously, of Tom Thurnall, and of Lancelot in *Yeast;* and socially, of everybody. But for and in himself, when I knew him, he was staunch to Church and State —'an old-fashioned High Churchman,' as I heard him define himself; 'an exact theologian,' as Sir William Cope defined him — and in manner he was the man of a generation more chivalrous, noble, and dignified than his own.

Such was the man that the victory of a stormy life well fought, and the wisdom of a fervid mind well disciplined, had made Charles Kingsley when I knew him.

When I left the stage and went to Cambridge, it was Canon Kingsley who, with my brother, assisted me to the step. His generosity and kindness were unfailing and true. In all mistakes I made, errors and follies not a few, he held his affection unwavering, always in touch with me, always understanding, sympathizing, harking forward. In very truth

> 'He tried each art, reproved each dull delay,
> Allured to brighter worlds, and led the way.'

Walking over the moor beyond and above the rectory one afternoon when I was last at Eversley, I called to mind happy walks with him. The remembrance of his words, of his habit of speech, the tone of his voice, and the influence of his presence, came very clearly to me. The afternoon was overcast; long lines of dun-coloured cloud were streaming over the Bramshill woods. The air was warm and moist and quiet. The colouring in the cloudy light was almost autumnal. On a moor the seasons are not very vividly marked by difference, save when the heather is in the full splendour of its bloom. The scene recalled to me an afternoon late in the year, when, walking across that very moor, Mr. Kingsley spoke words and suggested thoughts which made me always suppose he was in the mood which found voice and expression in that perfect and pathetic prose-idyll, *The Air Mothers.*

Two points I venture to think have not been sufficiently dwelt on with regard to Mr. Kingsley, even in the many pages that have, from time to time been written about him. These points are his poet-nature and his sense of humour. This poet-nature seems to me the clue to all his power and influence. It also explains, I think, certain qualities which exact scholars and accurate scientists sometimes called him to account for in his work. Over it all—theology, history, and science—as well as over its proper field of literature, the poet-nature seemed to dominate his utterance and thought. It gave a subtle charm to his work; touched it, indeed,—as it must be confessed the poet-nature, if deep and true, must always touch all work—with a life which the world recognizes as something of great value,—of, indeed, the greatest value. That his work was thus touched with life is, I think, clear. And a good proof of it—all the more convincing because so plain and practical—is that his work lives, possesses an altogether surprising vitality, and holds its own even in these busy days, and after the silence of death has so long passed between the world and him. The sale of his books remains enormous—almost beyond precedent.

Of his humour but little has been said. Yet it was the constant presence of this quality which made him such a delightful companion, and gave to his conversation its unfailing charm. But for his impediment in speaking, he would have been the finest talker I ever heard. At the rectory dinner-table I have seen very distinguished men gathered from time to time, but none could carry the palm of bright 'table-talk' away from Mr. Kingsley. And I think the most conspicuous quality of it was an ever-present trenchant humour.

It asserted itself at odd moments sometimes. I recall how that once when I had returned from Cambridge, I had to confess to various follies which were really almost as inexplicable (even to myself) as they were blameworthy. He listened with that strange power of sympathy he possessed—a sympathy all the more moving because you were conscious that by its side moved a stern and just integrity which would not be squeamish in condemnation of what was wrong. But before the latter feeling found words, he said, holding my arm with his strong, kind hand, 'Ah! of course, my dear boy, I understand. I know all about it. Yes. You can't eat your cake and have it too, can you? And you thought you would like to eat it. Well, there's a good deal to be said for that. A cake gets stale very soon. I dare say I should have done just the same in your place. After all you thought a cake is made to be eaten, isn't it? and it's very nice when it's new. Well, there it is. It's eaten—and now,' etc.

We were walking on the road to Bramshill with X——, a remarkably intelligent man, who had been discovered by Mr. Kingsley, and educated at his cost, and subsequently made his parish clerk and schoolmaster. The conversation turned on the subject of local ornithology. X—— said something to the effect that the bird he wished to see was a bustard. Mr. Kingsley stopped, and with the utmost gravity replied, 'My dear Fred, if you really wish to see a bustard, you must go to the marshes of Pomerania.' We all received the remark, X—— included, as gravely as it was delivered. It was only afterwards that the unintentional humour struck us. Probably X—— had made few journeys in his life beyond Wokingham or Reading, or, at most, London—thirty miles off. But Mr. Kingsley always courteously assumed that people could do what was desirable to be done. He widened horizons for every one, and made people feel free of the universe. That was his way. And there can be little doubt that, in most cases, it was a way that did good, and made men happier and better.

We were dining at Bramshill with Sir William Cope. There was a large party, to meet Bishop Wilberforce, who had lately come to Winchester. The conversation was very brilliant. A remark of Mr. Kingsley's specially delighted the bishop. They were talking about the Irish Church, which had then been recently disestablished, and had hurriedly proceeded to make sweeping changes in the order of the Prayer-book. The bishop and others were deeply lamenting the fact. 'It is,' said Mr. Kingsley, 'like the behaviour of a man who, having been with his goods violently ejected from his house in a thunderstorm, should take that opportunity of rearranging the furniture.'

Mr. Kingsley and I were walking in one of the Eversley lanes one day, when we met an old ne'er-do-weel of the parish. The rector stopped him; he stopped also the stream of maudlin words that the old fellow began to pour out. He talked kindly to him—kindly, but sternly, and yet, as it seemed to me, with a sort of deference, which under the circumstances was rather surprising. When we went on, he said, 'My dear Clifford, I am sorry to say it, but that old gentleman is a perfect blackguard. It's a very painful thing to say, but I am afraid he is what may be defined as rotten. I haven't a worse character in the place. He has lost everybody's respect, even —God help him!—his own. That is why I am so anxious to try and act as if he had not lost mine. Something may be done for him yet, if we can only show him that somebody is really interested in him. He may begin to think that God too, after all, is interested in him.' After a pause I said, 'Many people would like to know that. If we could only know that He really is interested.' 'We do know it!' he said, with wonderful earnestness; 'we do know it! Yes. I am sure of it, or, rather, I believe it, and that is better. I believe it with a faith that is surer than what we call knowledge. If I did not I could not keep sane in a world that then were a madhouse!'

Whenever Mr. Kingsley touched on a matter of faith, even as in the foregoing fragment of conversation, his earnestness was very striking. Into the very pronunciation of sacred words, and of names highest and holiest to one who loved to say, as he did, 'Before all things I am a priest,' he put a surprising vigour and life—a vitality so real that it arrested attention as to something new, and fraught with deep and daily personal interest. His reverence in conducting the Church service impressed every one who saw it. At times it touched on a solemnity that was contagious and unquestionable. In ordinary conversation he as little shrank from introducing and employing the names of Divinity as he was free from any touch of professional familiarity with them. And always the mere word 'God' seemed on his lips to hold a confessed and accredited sovereignty. It took the mind at once with a sense of illimitable power. It was no conventional word. It was alive, and exerted an influence over speaker and listener.

He was constantly looking at the skies, the

clouds, the stars. To hear him talk of them was in itself a poem. For the poet and the scientist met in him, and each enriched the store of the other. His power of expression was ready, and his vocabulary singularly large and varied. I remember one frosty night when the sky was brilliant with stars, his words rose to a height of wonderful eloquence in speaking of the old Greek myths and the eternity they seem to possess—starred as they are across the very heavens. The atmosphere and the clouds were absorbingly interesting to him. He was fond of prophesying the weather, and no one was more amused than himself to find the prophecies seldom fulfilled. 'A little knowledge is a dangerous thing,' he said to me one morning when he had foretold a fine day. 'We are often wrong, because as yet we know so little about the laws. That little may be right, but there is so much more to learn before we can apply it rightly. At present I am bound to say our knowledge is so little that it is a most dangerous thing—not to carry an umbrella'!

His love for science never for a moment seemed to mar or dispute the poetic and artistic love for Nature. The attitude of the man who wrote *The Water Babies* was preserved to the last. The running stream was an open book to him, not only of scientific, but also of fairy lore. He could tell us all about the little hidden waterfall that filtered its way through the rocks of Snowdon: and could with equal pleasure kneel down by the side of it where it tinkled against the stone, and cry with the delight of a child, 'Listen! Listen to the fairy bells!'

On some such occasion my brother asked him if his scientific knowledge had not dulled the splendour, and dissipated much of the mystery that fills the world to the poet's eyes. A very sad and tender look came over his face, and for a little while he was silent. Then he said, speaking slowly,—'Yes, yes, I know what you mean. It is so. But there are times—rare moments—when nature looks out at me again with the old bride-look.'

To any one who knew and loved Charles Kingsley, it is almost tiresome to find how many people think of him in his attitude towards nature solely as the singer of the *Ode to the North-West Wind*. That ode may be said to occupy the same relation to him as a poet that *Good News from Ghent* does toward Browning.

Both poems have gained a popularity that almost hurts their authors. In the case of Kingsley's ode, I suppose it is the unusualness of the subject which has made its notoriety, quite as much as the vigour and lilt of the picturesque lines. But no man could be more open to the softer and more delicate appeals of Nature than Kingsley. And for one day when he was in the mood that cried 'Welcome, wild North-Easter!" there were twenty when his heart sang, ' Oh that we two were maying, Over the fragrant leas!'

'Don't go out to-day,' I remember his once saying to me. '' This is a day that means to do people just as much harm as it possibly can. There is a wind' (it was from the northeast) 'that will kill you if you give it the chance. And you must take care that it doesn't take the chance without the giving. It is an assassin.'

Looking over some photographs of bleak and barren mountain ranges in the ' Western Avernus,' he said to me, 'Yes, aren't they hideous? Paint them, and send the picture to the Academy, and call it " The Abomination of Desolation."'

After he returned from the West Indies he

seemed to revel in the quiet, ordered, homely beauty of English landscape, although his pages of *At Last* show with what feeling of appreciation he had looked on the sights of the tropics. Some of his last words told us that he found perfect beauty in his own home scene. 'Tell him,' he said, speaking of his son, tell him I am looking at the most beautiful scene I ever saw.'

I cannot resist quoting a passage from my brother's letter in the *Life and Letters of Charles Kingsley*, because it describes a scene I know so well, and an incident I remember, for my brother and I were the 'young men' referred to.

'Surely if ever room could be haunted by happy ghosts it would be his study at Eversley. There, every book on the many crowded shelves looked at him with almost human friendly eyes. And of books what were there not?—from huge folios of St. Augustine to the last treatise on fly-fishing. And of what would he not talk? Classic myth and mediæval romance, magic and modern science, metaphysics and poetry, Western Indian scenery and parish schools, politics and fairyland. And of all he could speak with vivid sympathy, with keen humour, and oftentimes with pathos and profound knowledge. As he spoke and quoted, he would constantly verify his words. The book wanted—he always knew exactly where, as he said, 'it lived'—was pulled down with eager hands, and he, flinging himself back, with lighted pipe, into his hammock, would read, with almost boy-like zest, the passage he sought for and quickly found. It was very impressive to observe how intensely he realized the words he read. I have seen him overcome with emotion as he turned the well-thumbed pages of his Homer, or read aloud the heroic story of Sir Humphrey Gilbert in his beloved Hakluyt. Nor did the walls of the study shut him in entirely, even at such moments, or make him forgetful of what was going on outside. "It's very pleasant," he would say, opening the door which led on to the lawn, and making a rush into the darkness, "to see what is going on out here." On one such occasion, a wild autumnal night, after the thrilling recital of a Cornish shipwreck he had once witnessed, and the memory of which the turbulence of the night had conjured up, he suddenly cried, "Come out! come out, and look!" We followed him into the garden, to be met by a rush of warm rain driving before a south-westerly gale, which roared through the branches of the neighbouring poplars and Scotch firs. There he stood, unconscious of personal discomfort, for the moment silent and absorbed in thought, and then exclaimed in tones of intense enjoyment. "Splendid! What a night! Drenching! This is a night when you young men can't talk, can't think, too much poetry!"'

That there was in him the possibility of fierce delight in the stronger and wilder phases of nature, there can be no question. He seemed to have in his own veins some of that 'Viking's blood' of which he sings, and it was stirred by the stress of wind and wave and weather. One of the secrets of his power doubtless lay in this virility which could so rejoice in its own strength. And doubtless also this was the more to be valued in his work, as so much of the poetry of the day was marked with the feminine rather than the masculine note.

If, too, it be true, as has been often said, that tenderness is a characteristic of the truly manly nature, is indeed to be found in its perfection— as apart from gentleness, affectionateness, kindness, or any such feelings—only in men of manful mould, it may be that this very fibre of vigour gave to Mr. Kingsley his extraordinary faculty of tenderness. I call it extraordinary, for I have never seen—save in one man, my father,—such a development of this part of the manly nature. Doubtless this had grown and evolved itself out of his life and experience. The Mr. Kingsley I knew was possibly a very different and much more matured and developed man than the Kingsley of the 'Parson Lot' days. But I can only speak of him as I knew him. And so I say that alike in manner, action, and face, I found a wonderful truth of tenderness in him. I have sometimes seen him with a 'faraway' look on his face, which, for penetrating pathos and tenderness I have never seen equalled in any one's face before or since. At such times it seemed as if the fierceness, and turmoil and passion of the long day had burnt down into a light as calm and hopeful as that of a summer evening, and as infinitely pathetic.

True poet at heart and in life, beauty was to him a thing to be sought in all things, and reverenced wherever it was found. 'Beauty is God's handwork,' he writes, 'a wayside sacrament. Welcome it in every fair face, every fair sky, every fair flower, every fair scene, and thank Him for it who is the Fountain

of all Loveliness.' To him it was truly a
symbol, a signature of what is divine. But
looking on it thus, he loathed with necessary
scorn any degradation of it, or any application
of its likeness to base uses. It must be for
him in everything—in religion, in art, and in
life—the beauty of light, of virtue, of freedom,
of health, of truth; in fact, the Beauty of
Holiness. This, I think, was his life-quest—
the Holy Grail for which he sought. As poet
and as priest, the Beatific Vision was sought by
him in all his work and thought and life. It
seems clear from his words that it was so.
And in that when he lay nigh unto death, in
the silence of 'one of his last nights on earth,
. . . conscious of no earthly presence,' he
called out, 'How beautiful is God!'—who
shall say that the highest revelation of the
highest spiritual life was not at the last accorded to him?

It has been my privilege, in the course of my
work, to meet many men of note. I regret
that I have so often omitted in my notes to do
more than chronicle the fact. Pressure of time,
and a very treacherous memory for events
and for conversation, have often made such

chronicling little more than bare statements, uninteresting for any general reading. In such cases I must unwillingly reject them. But of some of the remarkable people I have met I find scattered notes, which I gather together, though in some instances, I fear, the result will but poorly show the pleasure and satisfaction I have felt in meeting those whose names I thus record.

Browning was the most entirely sympathetic listener I have ever found amongst poets and men of letters. He always criticized a thing on its own grounds, and did not adopt his own professional point of view. He was markedly and unfailingly kind to me, and always gave me the advantage of his valuable opinion. I first met him at Mrs. Inwood Jones's, in Sloane Street, in 1878. It was one Sunday afternoon. I found the poet there when I arrived. Our hostess introduced me at once, saying that the Sunday before (he generally called on the Sunday afternoon) she had told him about me. 'Yes,' he said, in his courteous way, 'and we were going to renew the conversation this afternoon. But you cancel that pleasure by a greater.'

He advised me not to give disjointed scenes from plays; and strongly urged me to preface certain recitations with a few words of explanation, 'in the good old-fashioned way,' he said, 'you know "it is necessary to apprise the reader," etc. Never suppose your audience knows the poem you are going to recite. Get people into the right frame of mind before you begin.' I have found this of the greatest practical use. It makes just all the difference to some pieces. The audience is thereby prepared from the first word to enter into the poem. Without some hint of explanation many poems are half over before even an intelligent listener, to whom the poem is new, has seized the dramatic position or caught the atmosphere. Notably this is the case with some of Browning's own poems, such as *The Italian in England* and *My Last Duchess*. A slight sketch of the person who is speaking makes the recitation carry conviction from the very first line.

Soon after I had met Browning I wrote to him to ask him if I could get a copy of *Hervé Riel*, which was not then included in his works. He sent me the kindest letter, and a copy of the magazine in which it had appeared—Macmillan's, I think.

He was a very generous listener. 'I am

afraid I missed a good many words in that last piece,' I said to him one afternoon at a private recital. 'What does it matter?' he said; 'the words you exchanged were, after all, unimportant. You are generally accurate. But the drama, the portrayal of the emotion, are the chief things for you. When I listen to a recitation or a play, I criticize the method, the declamation, the action, first. I can read the printed page for myself, if I want unfaltering accuracy. I want you to give me something the printed page can't. You are by no means best when you are most accurate.'

It was always pleasant to me to see him amongst my audience, and it was a pleasure he very kindly often gave me. He never took his eyes off the speaker, and, from remarks he made to me, I know that he valued action and facial expression as due and valuable parts of the art of recitation. He by no means wished, as so many people of literary instinct apparently do, to drag it down to mere matter of elocutionary repetition.

One of the last times I met Browning I told him—after thanking him for a letter I had just received—that in the following Saturday's recital I was giving the whole of the first part from his works, and I ventured to say how much I should be pleased if he would come. But he told me that he made a point of never going 'to hear himself recited.' I could not resist saying, "I know why, Mr. Browning. You are afraid of hearing, *How they brought Good News from Aix to Ghent*. Now, if you come on Saturday, I promise you you shall not hear *that!*' He told me that it was true he was aweary of that same 'fragment,' and of the many questions he had to answer about it. 'Upon my word,' he said, 'I think it is the only bit of verse of mine most people know anything about. Certainly it is the only one that is ever recited.' Some time before that he had told me that, as I suspected, the incident of these popular verses is a purely imaginary one. It catches a flavour of history, and is 'truer than truth,' in a sense. But the good news, the siege, the ride, the easy entrance into a beleagured city, all mean this—that, being once at sea, lying in his berth, wind and wave running high, he longed to be on land, and on the back of a favourite horse, and thereon amused himself by stringing together lines that should catch the lilt and rush and action of a galloping horse.

He was surprised at what he called my
'daring' in reciting *Holy Cross Day, My Last
Duchess*, and *Saul*. And when I told him I
was going to give *Count Gismona*, he said,
'Pray don't! Mrs. Grundy will have a fit in
the front row of the stalls if you do, and there'll
be a panic, and she'll write to the *Times*, and
the Lord Chamberlain, and your charming
recitals will be prohibited.' I told him I was
not afraid, as Mrs. Grundy never came to hear
me at the Steinway Hall. 'Good gracious!'
he said; 'no wonder everybody else goes!
What a charming and delightful place! 'Please
always keep my seat reserved for me. I shall
come whenever I can.'

I append the letter for which I thanked him.

'19, Warwick Crescent, W.
'January 12, 1887.

'DEAR CLIFFORD HARRISON,

'I am greatly obliged to you for the
notice you have always taken of my poetry,
and the prominence you so flatteringly accord
it in your present series of recitals. I shall
certainly do my best to bring these under the
notice, in turn, of friends whom they may
interest; and I shall myself hope to be able to

profit by the tickets you so kindly send me—if
not always (Saturday afternoons having many
claims on my time), yet whenever engagements
permit. The range of your power is truly
remarkable, and I observe with great pleasure
that various poems, in which I have already
experienced it, will be repeated. It is unnecessary to add how sincerely I wish you the
success you deserve, and beg you to believe me,
  'Yours most obliged, and very cordially,
              'ROBERT BROWNING.'

*   *   *   *   *

'Brantwood, Coniston, Lancashire,
            'February 4, 1885.

'MY DEAR SIR,
        'It is one of the most sure conditions
of my life, and I believe, if they noticed it, of
most people whose lives are of any varied
character and impulse, to have lucky and un-
lucky days. This has been to me an extremely
white—even refulgent—day. And among the
warmest rays of it, shone on me this afternoon
(I had no time to read in the morning) your
letter to Mrs. Severn, saying my books had
helped you, and that you would come and
recite to me in May.
  'I have just written to another delightful

correspondent, who, respecting a projected pleasantness in May, had said she wished it was April now, that *I*—on general principles—wished every day were two between January and May. But my general principles were certainly a little shaken by your letter.

'In the mean time, I see you speak of showing your drawings to Mrs. Severn. Would you mind sending me one or two to look at here? I am deeply interested in observing the degree in which the faculties of music and intelligent eloquence express themselves in style of drawing.

'Believe me, my dear sir,
'Gratefully and respectfully yours,
'J. RUSKIN.'

'Brantwood, Coniston, Lancashire.
'February 9, 1885.

'DEAR MR. CLIFFORD HARRISON,
'I can only tell you to-day that your drawings are safe here, and that they have given me more delight than any I have seen for years. In many things you have given me a lesson; in light and shade you might lesson anybody, and in mountain-forest drawing. But I can't say more to-day, but that I am,
'Gratefully yours,
'J. RUSKIN.'

These two very pleasant letters heralded my meeting with Mr. Ruskin in the May of 1885. From boyhood, I had read his eloquent and noble pages with unfailing delight, I owed much to his influence. It was, therefore, in love and gratitude to him for all that he had shown and given me, that I looked forward to our meeting. Mrs. Arthur Severn had told him about me, and, as his first letter shows, it was through her kind words our personal friendship began.

When Mr. Ruskin was in town in May, he came to see my mother and me one afternoon, and stayed with us for a long and delightful visit. We had a long talk about many things. I think that what most struck me was his ready sense of humour. I was surprised to find it so large an element in his conversation. I was prepared to hear beautiful thought clothed in beautifully chosen words; prepared, too, for occasional outbursts of well-defined dislike; even sometimes for a curious unworldly simplicity, which would fit in but ill with the angles of real life. But I was not prepared for such a constant and delightful sparkle of humour—a humour so ever present that it is often turned against himself, and can be amused at his own somewhat sweeping judgments. This makes his conversation always fresh and bright.

We naturally talked of my work. His courtesy led us quickly to it, and he expressed the truest interest. But I soon discovered— what subsequently, for my own judgment at least, I realized—that the interest was purely theoretical, and in great measure literary. It was the matter more than the manner that was of importance to him. Indeed, we had then, and afterwards, interesting discussions on this point. Acting and dramatic speaking had always, as it seemed, greatly interested him, and he had seen and heard the best actors and speakers of his day. He had theories about them. But I noted in all opinions he expressed, there was a deprecation of the executive art, and a desire to draw it back, as it seemed to me, into the parent creative art. It is curious how few men, even amongst the greatest, preserve entirely a true sense of the proportion and relation of things, and the application of universal laws. Rules are admitted to be true and necessary in this art, but are pronounced to be wholly untrue and unnecessary in that. No man alive has more emphasized the vital necessity for care, for study, for reverent finished work in painting and in architecture than Mr. Ruskin. The one thing he will not away with is haphazard, even when it comes with a fair title to the name of genius. Irreverent, careless, rough work cannot be tolerated. No; work—even when it seems most facile and sketchy—must be the result of forerunning care and thought; the liberty of a master hand, not the false 'boldness' of the tyro. One may almost venture to say he has been over-stern on this point, and has accentuated the condemnation of 'boldness' with something like invective. Yet I noted that this very 'boldness' was, apparently, what he liked on the stage and in reciting. In speaking of great actors, he nearly always brought against them the charge of artificiality. They were not 'natural,' not 'spontaneous' enough ; they had 'thought about it all too much.' This he said most emphatically about Macready whereby challenging a little good-natured argument with my mother. After he had heard me recite, he told me that my reciting was 'all too studied,' was not 'natural enough;' that he was sure I should recite much better if I did not learn my pieces, or think them out in every tone and gesture, but just took the book up and read them dramatically, as I felt at the moment. I pointed out to him that this was in effect the very denial of all his pet theories in another art; this was haphazard slapdash, rough art with a vengeance. But he said the matter was essentially different. No such parallel could be drawn. And on further talk I discovered the real reason of all this, namely, that recitation, and in a sense acting, was but a voice of literature to him; not *per se* an art. One piece which I recite notably raised Mr. Ruskin's ire. It was Adelaide Anne Procter's *Legend of Bregenz*. In vain I pointed out to him its unquestionable picturesqueness and drama, the opportunities for dramatic speaking, and the simple, clear way in which the legend is told. This last point was too much. He utterly denied its being an old legend, or having any historic or legendary value. I had not my facts to hand, so could not combat this. He remembered the discussion, and referred to the cause of it in one of his letters, in the following deliciously stated language:—

'Bother those recitations! That's what

makes you draw so badly!—telling horrid lies about girls swimming the Rhone on horseback, and the like bosh!'

The question raised, however, as to whether the story was a 'horrid lie' or not, made me inquire about it. Miss Douglas Galton hearing me speak of it, and finding herself subsequently at Lake Constance, went with some friend to Bregenz, and sent me a letter with the result of her search. She wrote, 'We were enchanted with Bregenz. . . . We verified the legend entirely, and I saw the carving of the girl and the horse over the old gateway. Every year in October they have a service in the church, and call out the maiden's name, and the name is "Gottien Epona."'

The point on which Mr. Ruskin and I really foregathered heartily, and with unity of interest and love, was drawing: and I need not say that on this point I listened to his words with absolute, unquestioning reverence. In any work I might attempt—drawing, painting, or music—I should never shrink from the judgment of a great artist, a real master of the art concerned. Such a man is always the most generous, and the most encouraging of critics. Of course he sees the faults. But if there be any spark of life in the work, any even latent life, I think he is sure to see it also. And *that* is the point he will see first. The merciless and hopeless critics are the mediocre folk, and, still more, the self-assured amateurs. When I had a request from Ruskin to send my drawings, I sent a portfolio off at once with delight. The result justified my trust. He gave me the best and brightest encouragement I have ever had. He also, of course, told me of my faults as no one ever had. Both were great gifts. The latter, from such a man, is indeed the more valuable of the two.

I have, unfortunately, mislaid some letters I greatly prized, but of those I have I must quote two or three, as being characteristic of the writer and his warm-hearted interest, and because they are so pleasant and valuable to me.

'Brantwood, Coniston, Lancashire,
'November, 1885.

'DEAR CLIFFORD,

'I am ashamed to have kept your drawings so long. . . . For the drawings of Alpine wooded mountains are a pleasure to me such as no man ever gave me before; and the light and shade is a lesson to me in the management of half-tints such as I never got before, and which I haven't got to the bottom of yet. On the other hand, there are humours and faults in you that are inscrutable to me. First, that you take no interest in architecture as such. You are as content with a horse-trough as with the Castle of Chillon, if you like the light and shade and sentiment. And yet you can't do without architecture in its domestic character. You stay days and days drawing the ivy up a garden wall, but in all your drawings there isn't a single grand natural foreground rock with ivy up *its* wall. And then, with all your heaven-born feeling and mortal-born skill, you won't take pains enough to learn to draw a water-butt, or half a crown, in perspective—how much less a boat!

'When next we meet, I'll be—whatever the Fates like to say—if I don't make you draw a tub in perspective for once!

'Ever marvellingly yours,

'J. RUSKIN.

'P.S.—You are cruelly, inexcusably, and unpardonably careless to draw things back to back, and then knock and shuffle them about the world.'

'Brantwood, Coniston, Lancashire,
'January, 1886.

'Dear Clifford,

'You cannot conceive—nay, I will not say that—but, at least, I can't tell you the joy I had in hearing the Glacier des Bossons was restored. I thought it was gone for ever, and that perhaps the Alpine snows would vanish altogether, and that the modern world would enter on a new epoch of lightless hills.

'If I'm spared I'll see the Glacier des Bossons once more before I die. Can you tell me what state the Glacier des Bois was in? It has been a mere thread on the top of its precipice for the last ten years.

'It is a lovely drawing, that Bossons. But are you sure you could not colour? With your sense of mountain majesty, how you would rejoice in painting them! And then think, green ice and blue water; and me, oh, so happy!

'Ever your grateful,
'J. Ruskin.'

'Brantwood, Coniston, Lancashire,
'October, 1886.

'DEAR CLIFFORD,

'I return from Switzerland in sorrowfully returning your beautiful drawings. I could not part with them sooner; nor could I sooner write of them, for I had much to think of in the course of your work. Progressive, in some directions, it is; yet it is weaker than the sepia work. The friends are right for once in saying, don't change your style. For one thing, it is a principle in all art never to do laboriously what can be done easily; and all pencil is misused which only does what sepia could do better.

'. . . But you will work past all this. You must study Turner's pencil work. . . .'

'Brantwood, Coniston, Lancashire.

'DEAR CLIFFORD,

'. . . I am not allowed to write after my day's work now, except the merest scraps to my best friends. But I must hope to get power of petition enough into this scrap to get me a loan of some more drawings. You must not send them about to people—not to anybody but me. And you must take great care in handling them yourself, which I know you won't do. But pencil is the only proper sketching-tool; and, of course, exactly the one the modern tribe of daubers and scratchers hate the sight of; . . . and this summer you must paint, nothing but paint.

'Your loving,
'J. R.'

It is a great pity that my memory for some things is so bad. I forget conversations and observations that I hear. I have thus lost much of interest before I could find time to record it in my note-books. But once I remember talking with Mr. Ruskin about war and soldiers, and he said, 'Ah! all my life I have inveighed against war as possibly the most entirely wicked and inhuman thing in the world. I have called it and its ministers the worst of names, and have evolved the most tremendous of theories about it and them; and I am bound to say that some of my dearest friends, and many of the men who have best fulfilled my ideal of gentle manhood—simple, strong, godly, and true—have been soldiers. That ought to teach me to be reticent, ought it not? But it hasn't.'

Almost the last letter I have received from him, ended thus:

'. . . This may catch you at your work, or follow you home, or lose itself. Then I'll write a better one. Only please tell me as much as ever you like of anything you'd like to tell me always.

'Your ever affectionate,
'J. RUSKIN.'

At Mr. Hamilton Aïdé's charming rooms I have met (as who that has the *entrée* there has not?) many interesting people. No parties are pleasanter, both socially and artistically, than those which gather at his hospitable bidding. It was in his rooms that I first gained the good praise of Browning, of Matthew Arnold, of Frederick Locker, and of Mrs. Fanny Kemble. Hamilton Aïdé gave me a piece of his own to recite that year, which became my chief dramatic recitation. It was unpublished, and it is always a great gain to have a piece that is not known, and cannot be appropriated instantly by that noble army of reciters which is ever ready to rush from afar to new ground. The poem, *George Lee*, affords great scope of drama for the reciter.

I used to recite several of Frederick Locker's delicate and dainty verses. No writer, save perhaps Austin Dobson, has given us more charming *vers de société* than Mr. Frederick Locker, and many of his little poems lend themselves admirably to recitation. He was very kind to me. One evening, at his request, I went to Lord Tennyson's to be introduced to the poet, who received me with the kindest courtesy, and bade me come and see him.

I called on him early the following season. Directly I appeared, Mr. Tennyson (it was in 1881) asked me what line it was I wanted to ask him about. This was rather perplexing, as I came with no such question ready. However, I was able to tell him that I was going to recite the oath-scene from *Harold* that night at a recital out of London; and that I had recited *The Defence of Lucknow* at a house in Warwickshire where Lord Hertford was staying, and that he was profoundly affected by the noble lines. We spoke of our 'mutual friend,' Mrs. Greville, whose recitation of *The Grandmother* was really an excellent piece of drama. He asked me what pieces of his I liked reciting best, and I told him, *The Lotus Eaters* first, then *The Brook*, and *Amphion*, and *Locksley Hall*. He spoke about *The Brook* in a way that made me think it was a pet child of his. I told him also that for a long recitation no piece affords such variety of drama, and has such an unfailingly great effect on an audience as *Enoch Arden*. He spoke with some bitterness about his plays not being acted, having been written for the stage. That year and the following year Lord Tennyson asked me several times to his house, and I retain the most grateful and pleasant recollection of his invariable kindness. When I published a little volume of verses, he sent me, through Mr. Hallam Tennyson, the most pleasant and encouraging message; and when I began my first long series of recitals in London I received, on the morning of the first recital, this kindly remembrance—

'DEAR SIR,
    'My father is unable to write to you to-day, but bids me say that he wishes you all success in your recitations. . . .
            'HALLAM TENNYSON.'

Mr. Hamilton Aïdé took me to Mrs. Fanny Kemble one evening for a reading of *Romeo and Juliet.* I had met her at his rooms a short time before (December, 1879) and recited to her. She was kind and encouraging in her judgment.

I remember that I was dreadfully nervous at going to read the part over with her, although I was delighted beyond words at the chance of hearing her read. It was a great privilege, and one I think of with lively pleasure and gratitude. But, as she said to me, 'I owe my friend Mr. Aïdé acquiescence to any request of his, and he has asked me to do this.' She subsequently wrote, 'How little the process you endured the other night was likely to be of use to you I am afraid I can judge, but I should have been heartily glad to have served you if I could.'

The fear I felt at the ordeal was not lessened when I entered her presence, and, with few words of greeting, she plunged at once into the matter in hand, and gave me my cue.

' " Good morrow, cousin ! " '

Faintly I replied, ' " Is the day so young ? " '

'Good heavens! you're never going to say it like that!' she exclaimed.

I turned cold with agitation.

But after this alarming beginning I soon

became enthralled. I did not try to do my
part well. I could only listen and note. In
vain she asked me to go through certain scenes;
I was a dummy. But it did not matter. The
thing was to listen to her. It seems to me
that it was magnificent speaking. The scansion
of the lines were occasionally disregarded, and
Garrick's edition of the play was followed. As
a bit of drama, and of dramatic speaking, I have
never heard anything finer. She said that of
course as a poem Shakespeare's play is perfect;
but Garrick, being a great actor, knew his art
and proved his knowledge when he altered the
play. 'You know,' she said, 'what I think of
the stage, and of acting as an art; we need not
argue that. But I know what acting demands
and what the stage requires, and I say Garrick
knew what he was about when he altered such
and such lines, and remoulded the catastrophe,
bringing it back, remember, to the original tale.
Shakespeare, with true poet's art, altered the
end, and made Romeo die before Juliet recovers—die, thinking his lady-love is dead.
The original tale makes Juliet recover from
her trance before Romeo dies. This Garrick
restored, seeing how fine a situation this is for
the stage. I have played both; my father has

played both; and I *know* which is best for the stage.' Then she said, 'Remember this curious fact. Shakespeare gives the sentiment, the poetry, the affectionateness of love to Romeo—the man. The passion of love he gives to Juliet.'

She told me that her father's 'banishment scene was magnificent. His bursts of passion were always fine, she said; but he could not sustain long tragedy. In this 'banishment scene, as she described it, 'it was with him the exhibition of sheer despair. And after he heard of Juliet's death, everything was drowned in grief. There was not a tone, a gesture, a look that forgot that absolute life-weariness.'

Mrs. Fanny Kemble read many of the scenes. After the weak, unimpassioned, yet over emphasized delivery which we hear so often nowadays on the stage, when a line of blank verse will sometimes be cut up into little accentuated groups of two and three words, it was a pleasure to hear the words roll grandly along through all the line. It seemed to portray a generosity of passion which rendered the fervour of the diction and the dignity of verse but its natural and inevitable expression. With her it was the drama and force of the emotion that was expressed; not the mere picturesque power of certain words and phrases that was verbally accentuated. When she had finished the reading she was much excited, and her hand quite shook with emotion. 'You see,' she said, 'I was never a real actress. I always felt the part too much. Great art feels once and deeply, and then reproduces and spiritualizes the exact portrayal of the feeling. I feel it all too much. Go and play, and let me get a little quieted again.'

A few days afterwards I received a letter and enclosure from Mrs. Fanny Kemble, from which I make the following extracts:—

'... I send you a few hasty notes upon the part, which I have jotted down for your consideration. If you would like me to mark a common stage copy of the play for you after our old fashion of acting, I shall be glad to do so.
'Yours very faithfully,
'FRANCES ANNE KEMBLE.
'I owe you many thanks for your music, which gave me great pleasure, and *rested* me.'

'Advice of an old actress of the Antediluvian Classical School to a young gentleman thinking of going on the stage.

'Indispensable acquirements: to know how—

'To stand quite still;

'To move your hands and arms without your feet and legs;

'To move your feet and legs without your hands and arms;

'To move your whole body;

'To dance well;

'To fence well;

'To play singlestick well;

'To articulate words from one syllable to six progressively;

'To read prose, poetry, and blank verse;

'To declaim prose, poetry, and blank verse.

'After acquiring absolute proficiency in all these things, you may begin to study for the stage.

'You will observe that these are all mere physical qualifications. The intellectual one I have not touched on.'

'Notes upon Romeo.

'Romeo represents the sentiment, Juliet the passion, of love. The pathos is his, the power hers.

'His first scene is mere rose-light before sunrising. The key-note of the after real love and life is given in the lines, "I fear too early."

'The spirit of the balcony scene is that of joyful tenderness and something of a sort of sweet surprise at the fervid girl-passion which suddenly wraps him round and carries him, as with wings of fire, toward the level of its own intensity.

'All the succeeding scenes are pervaded by the elastic spirit of the joy and triumph of his secret happiness. Mercutio's death is the heavy thunder-cloud in the bright sky; his own duel with Tybalt, the breaking of the lightning flash and the falling of the bolt that strikes. His furious burst of uncontrolled rage and hatred is followed by utter collapse of all passion, leaving him consciousness, but not discrimination, of infinite trouble, a nightmare of measureless misery.

'The scene in the Friar's cell is the sheer expression of the violence of weakness. Hunted for his life by the Capulets; hidden from the pursuit of public justice; palpitating with nervous anguish; horror of his sanguinary deed, because the victim is kinsman to his wife; passionate longing and desire for the possession of that wife, for which all preparation had been made, even for that night;—the spirit of the whole scene is summed up in the speech beginning, "Thou canst not speak of what thou dost not feel." Gradually, as the friar utters his consolatory admonition, the vital invincible hope of youth, and the anticipation of the "joy past joy" which beckons him, rise victorious above all his wretchedness, and culminate in the farewell.

'The parting scene in Juliet's room is languid with passion, wan with woe. Beneath the reiterated tender offering of his life to her, the throbbing of the natural desire to live again asserts itself. Here again his self-sacrifice is the sentiment, her selfishness the passion, of love.

'The opening of the fifth act is a gentle melancholy, a blending of exquisite memories and of hope, in a pervading atmosphere of profound sadness.

'After the news of her death comes one blasphemous outburst of mad agony, and then the iron gloom of utter despair, through which he dwells, strangely enough, on the details of the apothecary's shop and existence, with one or two sobs of softer sorrow. His farewell to

Balthazar, his warning to Paris, his recognition of him after killing him, are all lingering and broken touches of the sweet, tender, pathetic nature that is choked with bitterness of fate, and sinking fast to the blackness of despair and death.'

'I am not careless, as I may have appeared to you, of the value of the text of Shakespeare. But poet, philosopher, and playwright as he was, your dealings with him would be in the latter capacity only. You need not be afraid of eliminating the two nobler elements of his work. Omit what you will, *that* is impossible. Remember, too, that his inspiration (and I use the word advisedly) did not protect him from the errors of his time and place. As for occasional breaking of his lines, my excitement the other evening made it more frequent than it would have been had I been more mistress of myself. But there are faulty lines in Shakepeare, and a good musician should know how to redeem such, in some measure, by his mode of rendering them.

'FRANCES ANNE KEMBLE.'

I recited once before George Eliot, but it

was in a private room, and at a rather crowded party—the sort of reciting I most dislike, and can do least well. I remember how narrowly she watched me. I had a feeling that she knew how I felt. When it was over she said, 'I am glad to have heard you, if that can be called a hearing; but I am sure I cannot judge.' I value the remembrance of some measured words of praise she gave me. 'But,' she said, 'I wonder you consent to recite under such circumstances. Why do you do it?' I explained that it was difficult sometimes to refuse. I seemed uncivil, perhaps even unkind. 'Yes, I dare say it is hard,' she said; 'but any one who wants to make his work artistic has to seem—and perhaps to be—very hard sometimes.'

I never saw any one whose face was so altered and illuminated by a smile. But even in repose her face was to my eyes far too remarkable to be plain. There is a beauty of plainness just as there is surely an insignificance, not to say negation of beauty, in some 'good looks.'

There is no author whose humour I enjoy reciting better than George Eliot's.

I first had the pleasure and the privilege of

meeting Dean Stanley in 1873. My brother then held a minor canonry at Westminster, and I was living with him. It was a memorable thing to be shown over the Abbey by Dean Stanley. He knew every corner, and could narrate its history in the most interesting and picturesque way. I remember once his taking a party of friends over. We were four hours in the Abbey, Cloisters, and Chapter House, yet the time seemed short. It was very curious that he should have had such a faculty of picturesque description at such a time, for I believe he owned to being what is called colour-blind, and certainly he had no ear for music. Yet when he recalled the scenes of the historic and stately Abbey church, and painted with graphic words its memories and pageants, there seemed neither lack of colour nor indifference to the appeal of sound in the pictures drawn. His description of the opening of the vault where Mary Queen of Scots lies, and of the coffin of Richard II., was extraordinarily impressive.

'Colour-blindness' is confessed to be a very difficult thing to prove, but of the 'ear for music' it is easier to make a test. I have heard the late Dean of Westminster confess that he could not recognize any tune, except perhaps—if association suggested it—*God save the Queen!* I have also heard him say that the drum was the instrument he liked best! But I think the most curious statement with regard to sound I ever heard was one he made when describing the riots that took place many years ago at St. George's-in-the-East. A disorderly mob used to besiege the church to protest against, and to try to turn into ridicule, the ritual that was instituted there. The scene must have been shocking in every way. During the Absolution the mob would shout out the words in every tone of insult and anger. It would be hard to conceive anything worse in the way of bad noises than the roar of an angry, blasphemous crowd. Yet Dean Stanley, describing it, said 'No; it was really very fine—a wonderful noise, like the sound of many waters.'

Of all handwritings I have seen I think the most illegible was that of Dean Stanley. I believe that he owned that on more than one occasion he was quite unable, when in the pulpit, to decipher his own sermon. Once when I was staying at the Cloisters, and my brother was away from home, a letter was brought to me from the Deanery. The butler who brought it said that it was important, and that he was to wait for an answer. I studied the hieroglyphic enclosed. After five minutes of frantic pursuit after revelation, I was fain to run to the Deanery and plainly tell the Dean that I couldn't make out a word. He was extremely amused, and as kind as he always was, and I was able to answer verbally the question which had 'assumed such dark disguise' on paper.

I remember, too, that once at Eversley Rectory, Canon Kingsley received a letter from the Dean. Mrs. Kingsley was very ill at the time. The letter arrived at dinner-time, by the evening post. Mr. Kingsley opened it, and examined it for many minutes. At last he said, 'I have every reason to believe that this is a very kind letter of sympathy from Stanley. I feel sure it is. Yet the only two words I can even guess at are "heartless devil"! But I pause—I pause to accept that suggestion, as scarcely likely one under the circumstances.'

One of the last times I met Dean Stanley was at Alford House one afternoon. The Crown Prince and Princess of Prussia had been lunching with Lady Marian Alford. I was to recite several pieces after luncheon.

Before I began, the Dean of Westminster came up and asked me if he could do anything to help me, as to where I should like to stand, where people might sit, etc. He was so interested, as he most kindly and cordially said, in my work. I am quite sure he meant it. But his power of observation in small practical matters was limited, as I knew well. I was not, therefore, wholly surprised when, in the middle of my second recitation, he got up, crossed the room, took away the chair I had placed near (as I wanted to use it in the action of the recitation), and sat down on it, quite close up to me, just as if he was going to be part of the performance. I believe it was all done with an earnest wish to mark great attention and special interest, and he was quite unconscious that the method of doing so was nearly as disturbing to the audience as it was to me. When I had finished, there could be no doubt of his wish to mark his approbation or as to the kind and gracious way in which it was expressed.

On this occasion (at Alford House) I had the honour of being presented to the late Empero Frederick and to the Empress Victoria (the Crown Prince and Princess of Prussia). H impressed me as having the finest manners I have ever seen—absolute grandeur, at once simple, unaffected, and dignified. After I had recited my own verses of *The Signalman*, he came up to me, shook hands with me in the most cordial manner, and thanked me. 'I have seldom heard anything that moved me more,' he said. 'The tale is a noble one.' I informed his Imperial Highness that it was a true story, and told him about it. 'I think the man was quite right,' he said; 'I am a soldier, and a father also, but he was right. . . . You should have a good career. . . . That must be better, much better, to recite to public audiences. I am glad to hear you do that. You cannot care for such audiences as you get in private rooms. You ought always to speak in public; but I am glad you do not always, or I should not have heard you to-day. I wish you success.'

Being the chief of all the dunces, I am, as a rule, far from feeling at home when I find myself with scholars. Therefore it is all the more delightful and memorable when I meet a scholar in whose presence I find such kindly charm that I forget my ignorance. Such I found in Dr. Vaughan, when I once had the pleasure of staying for two days at the Deanery, Llandaff. There are men who do not impress you with the fact of their own cleverness so much as that for the time being, whilst you are with them, they seem to raise you to their own level. Canon Kingsley was a perfect example of this; and I found in the Master of the Temple the same beneficent and admirable power. He was far more than the mere scholar. If he were not, I for one should have been tongue-tied, frozen, dumb, before him. I have an almost measureless admiration for scholasticism; but I have also a bitter envy of it, and an inborn antagonism to it. And this mental trio—by no means an unusual combination—dispute for my body when I find myself in the presence of learning— learning of the encyclopædic and academic kind. I have always supposed that a course of public school masters, taken without due precaution, would kill me. For the scholar pure and simple is a Medusa's head to me, and turns me to stone. I never, however, felt less like stone than I did in that very comfortable household, under the walls of the old Welsh cathedral.

There was a recital at Cardiff one evening.

The Dean had a lecture to give, and so could not be present, which his courtesy enabled him to say he regretted. He is an excellent and entertaining talker, and his perfect pronunciation is a study in itself to any one interested in speaking. The pronunciation, indeed, is almost faultless, and, from the scholarly point of view, may be pronounced to be perfect.

Pleasant days in my work have given me few episodes more pleasant than a visit I once paid to Dr. John Brown, when I was in Edinburgh in the January of 1880. I thought myself very fortunate in seeing him, for there were, alas! many days when he could not see any one. But when I went, it was a happy hour: and the beautiful, almost saintly, lines of his face wore the look of peace and hope. We talked of many things and people, and notably of our dear friend, Lady Caroline Charteris, whose bright faith and active goodness seemed a fitting topic for him to speak of. He showed us some drawings by Turner, and some sketches by Leech; also a drawing of the beloved and now renowned 'Rab.'

'And are you two great friends?' he said, putting a hand on W.'s arm. 'That is right.

I like to hear it. An artist always has the faculty of friendship more than other men have.' I spoke with some enthusiasm, and probably a good deal of folly, on some question of art. 'Yes,' he said, 'but be careful of thinking too much about that same "Art" with a big A! Every age, I suppose, has its pet hobby, and the hobby-horse of this age, as far as I can see, is Art with a big A. It covers a multitude of sins nowadays, and is an excuse for a good deal of something I, being old-fashioned, should call Self-Will.' When I went away he wished me a Godspeed in my work, which he pleased and encouraged me by calling 'honourable and beautiful.' There was something about him—a sort of invisible nimbus of a homely kind—which gave such a valediction a very distinct meaning and value.

Another man of note I am very glad to have had the privilege of seeing and talking to, is Sir Henry Taylor. Lady Pollock took me to see him many years ago. He was living at East Sheen then. Subsequently I met him at Bournemouth. The first visit greatly interested me. Lady Pollock had kindly told him about my recitation of a scene from *Philip Van Artevelde*, which she considered the best thing

I had then done. We talked it over, and I told him that I had made a longer selection still from the second part of the play, including Artevelde's magnificent speech to the Herald, and the fine scene where he tells the Lady Elena about his dream. Sir Henry frankly owned that the play was a failure when Macready produced it. It was only played a few nights. He agreed with Lady Pollock that it was one of the great actor's finest impersonations. It seems inexplicable that so great a play thus acted, failed to hold its own on the boards. It must have been produced at an unfortunate time. Sir Henry said, 'The fault lay either with me or with the public, certainly not with the actor. I suppose it was my fault. The writing of an acting play seems to be almost a lost art.' I ventured to suggest that it was possible our modern poets had been, and were still, not willing enough to have their plays handled and manipulated by actors to gain popularity on the acting stage; that they refused to permit what used to be called Acting Editions of plays as opposed to Library Editions. Shakespeare himself presumably accepted this condition. Certain it is that most of his plays come down to us on the stage with all sorts of alterations for stage use, and with a mass of tradition, technical 'business,' and alteration. Was not the literary point of view of drama always in reality a different point of view from that of the actor's drama? And is it not true that almost all the great plays of literature which also hold the stage have been 'adapted'— possibly with the author's full consent—to the process of obedience to this second point of view? He naturally contested for the absolute integrity of the author's work, but added that it was to be remembered, as some argument for the other side, that Shakespeare had the rare advantage of being an actor as well as a poet. I confessed that it was my belief that some of the stage alterations in Shakespeare's plays may possibly have come down to us from the poet himself in stage tradition, and be parts of his practical acting editions of his own work. 'It is true,' said Sir Henry Taylor, 'that in some of the greatest ages of art artists themselves have had least thought as to the jealous "integrity" of art, and have been most indifferent as to processes of assimilation and alteration.'

When I went away, Sir Henry Taylor most kindly gave me his plays and poems, and wrote a word or two of gracious purport in the first volume. But it was something of a disappointment, as well as of amusement, to me, on getting the books home, to find that, in the hurry of the moment, he had linked my surname with the Christian (*sic*) prefix that, as a man of letters, would naturally first occur to him, and had inscribed the gift with all sincere and hearty good wishes to 'Frederick Harrison.'

There is no one whose 'Walks abroad' are more known, or are more generous of gift in pen and pencil, than those of Mr. Augustus Hare. No one is more at home in many homes than he is; no one knows 'the stately homes of England' better, or could better show in sketch-books and portfolios innumerable 'how beautiful they stand!' Yet his own beautiful little home, Holmhurst, betrays no desire to walk abroad, or disposition to change with days that are days of change. It wears, unaltered, unruffled, and secure, its own somewhat old-fashioned air and manner.

'Tempora mutantur, nos et mutamur in illis,' does not seem to hold good there. Nothing changes; nothing is changed. The very flowers in the pretty gardens reassert themselves year after year in position and colour. The house is a museum of interesting things. But everything has its place, and the place and it are one. Times may change, but Holmhurst changes in them just as little as it possibly can. Even that little change is deprecated. And when one goes for a pleasant visit there after an absence of three or four years, one seems to take up life exactly where one left it. To look at the perfectly ordered house and the grounds, you would think the master never walked abroad; whereas the question might with some show of reason be asked, when is he at home?

My note-books should have, by right, one of their best pages given to Holmhurst. For it was there, at the urgent advice of my friend Augustus Hare, that I determined to begin them. Augustus Hare himself has note-books which certainly are delightfully full of interest, social and literary, as perhaps the reading world will one day know. It was the great interest I expressed in hearing him read some of his pages that pointed his advice of imitation.

Everybody who knows Augustus Hare— and everybody does know Augustus Hare!— knows how wonderfully well he tells a ghost-story. He has a fine collection of ghosts. They are all labelled and certified with names, dates, and references—the most authenticated and documented ghosts I know. A ghost-story gains greatly by dramatic telling. Written down, it loses some of its 'creepiness.' Augustus Hare tells a story of a vampire which, in his hands, owes a good deal to the 'points of circumstance' with which he tells it. I have heard the tale also from a descendant of the possessors of Crogley Grange, in which house the grisly incident occurred, and the tale is undoubtedly full of curious and somewhat unanswerable questions.

Augustus Hare is the pleasantest of hosts. One is always amused at Holmhurst. The place is charming; there is plenty to do, and nothing 'to be' done; the conversation is unusually bright and gay, and the days are free from that burdensome programme of proposed 'amusement' which makes barren so many visits.

In the house there are many drawings by Flaxman, whose sister—in the last generation —was a governess in the family. There are, too, many relics of Pius IX.

Each generation, I suppose, has its own standpoint, and, in certain ways, its own fashion of life; yet to each there comes something of heritage from the generation passed away. The author of *The Memorials of a Quiet Life* can scarcely live the quiet life those Memorials tell us of, for they are the record of a time farther removed from ours than mere years can account for. That record tells us of lives highly cultivated and fully lived in all true ways of living—lives which, however, saw but little change, and to which certain walks in Tenby were a centre of eventful interest. The author of the records, himself the descendant of those whose lives he records, travels far and wide; and *Walks in Rome*, in Spain, in Northern Italy, and Southern France, are perhaps not more eventful or flavoured with adventure to him than was a journey to South Wales to those who live in the pages of the *Memorials*. The gulf between the generations is deep and wide, yet the practical heritage in this case seems clear and substantial. It is found at Holmhurst, and Augustus Hare preserves it reverently. The *Quiet Life*—for loss or gain—has passed away from the hands of this generation, but the *Memorials* remain: and we find them often in English country houses, and in cultivated, quiet, English home-life. One would be sorry to see the day when their signature is erased, and their influence lost or rejected.

I recited *The Story of the Faithful Soul* to music for the first time at Mr. Hamilton Aïde's one evening when Mrs. Procter was present. She was very encouraging in her criticism of my delivery of her daughter's well-known lines. 'But,' said she, 'the story is strangely sentimental, is it not? But then, Adelaide *was* sentimental!'

Certainly the quality was not hereditary. No one had a more keen, clear, critical faculty than Mrs. Procter. She was a wonderful woman. I believe she was of great age, but she looked bright and rosy and vivacious, and no one was more interested in life and society than she was almost to the last.

'And now,' she said, that same evening, 'I'm going to do what I never have done yet—find fault with you. Why do you recite Browning? I heard you give *Hervé Riel* the other day. It is impossible. It is all too involved—too obscure. Tell me, why do you recite it?'

We had an interesting talk about the matter. I tried to convince her that Browning, in certain poems, is essentially 'recitable;' that he lends himself to dramatic declamation, and gains by it. For sentences that on the page are involved and twisted, or broken by parentheses, in recitation grow lucid and clear; their very involved character fits them for dramatic speaking, for thus they become life-like utterances of an impersonated character. She promised to come and hear one of my Saturday afternoons, when I gave the first part of the recital from Browning.

P.S.—She never came.

I remember meeting Madame Mohl years ago at Lady Pollock's, and at Lady Castletown's. Once I suffered somewhat from her exuberant vivacity. It was before I had taken to reciting professionally. One day at a large luncheon-party at Lady Castletown's I was asked, after luncheon, to recite. Mr. Alexander Yorke had just recited *The Bells.* Directly I got up and announced that I had been asked to recite, Madame Mohl bustled up and said 'Well, I'll go!' and in a 'stage whisper' informed her neighbour, as she went away, that she did not care for amateur reciting. (She was a very clever woman.) I so deeply agreed with her in my heart of hearts that I found some difficulty in screwing up my courage to th sticking-point. Before two verses were finished Madame Mohl danced back into the room in her sprightly way. 'Don't let me interrupt anybody,' she said ; 'but my dear'—speaking to a lady near the door—be sure you're not later than ten. I shall be waiting.' And she disappeared again. I recommenced with what of spirit remained in me, when lo! again the door opened, and in waltzed the lively little old lady, and literally ran about the room. 'I'm so sorry,' she said ; 'don't let me interrupt anybody, but I've left my parasol somewhere. Don't mind me. Here it is! That's all right,' and again disappeared. But this was more than I could withstand. I sat down and said I was afraid I couldn't go on, etc., etc. The comedy of the situation was too much. Everybody agreed, and laughed and applauded. It was quite a success —the leaving off, I mean—thanks to Madame Mohl.

I remember reciting Walter Herries Pollock's adaptation of Alfred de Musset's *La Nuit d'Octobre* for the first time one evening at Lady Pollock's. There were many distinguished people there, and amongst them, conspicuous in interest to me, were Delaunay and Mounet

Sully. I wonder now at my courage on venturing to recite the piece before Delaunay. He was very civil, and gave me valuable hints. But it must have seemed a terribly crude performance to him, I fear. He could not follow the English, but he complimented me on the way I permitted the lines to run unbroken sometimes. He had been struck with the fact that so many English actors break up lines with verbal rather than with emotional drama, and he asked if this were necessary in English verse.

He gave a long recitation; and Mounet Sully recited a short poem very beautifully. Delaunay wore gloves all through the recitation, which greatly disturbed my English eye. I thought that he lost so much expression, too, by covering his hand. Also he moved about, changing his position in the room, as if in acting; which seemed to me to distract attention. But it was, of course, a fine performance, and a perfect bit of declamation.

Lady Pollock's drawing-room was the scene of one of my earliest attempts at reciting, or 'reading,' before I took to it professionally. We read together a scene from *The Spanish*

Gypsy (George Eliot), and one or two scenes from *Romeo and Juliet.* Her advice was very valuable. There is no better judge of reciting, as of acting, than Lady Pollock. Her faculty of criticism is as true as her friendship, and more can scarcely be said.

Her words of encouragement were the first of any weight out of my own home that I received. Years ago, soon after I left Cambridge, I gave a recital at the Beethoven Rooms. My dear college friend, Walter Pollock, wrote to his mother about me, and she went to hear me. The next morning I received a letter from her, giving a generous measure of praise—praise, indeed, so full, and so well-tempered by discerning and helpful criticism, that it remains to this day as one of my highest encouragements. Let me also briefly chronicle here the steadfast friendship I received from the late Sir Frederick Pollock. For nearly twenty years I had the privilege of knowing him, and I retain the brightest memory of the many delightful hours spent in his house, and of his unfailing and marked kindness. He used to collect the most interesting people at his table, and he was a charming host. No one could tell an anecdote with more humour and point. I have had the pleasure of meeting many remarkable and notable people at his table—Matthew Arnold, Sir Frederick Leighton, Browning, Kinglake, Henry Irving, Lord Houghton, and many others.

At one of these pleasant dinner-parties I remember Lord Houghton was very amusing. I suppose he was considered one of the best *raconteurs* of his day. Like many brilliant talkers, he necessarily at times dominated the table, and lesser mortals had to accept the parts of stage 'guests,' and content themselves with smiling and looking appropriate. But it was a pleasant part to play when Lord Houghton held the stage. In Sir Frederick Pollock Lord Houghton found a conversationalist worthy of his steel. I wish I could remember, and had been able to 'book,' some of the things said, but even did my memory serve me in such matters, good taste might forbid its exercise. I remember, however, that Lord Houghton told a story *à propos* of authors and publishers which was new to us, though he said it was well known.

It was at the time when the name of Buonaparte was a terror and execration to Europe.

At an annual dinner of a certain society of authors in London, Campbell (?) rose and said he had to propose a toast. Glasses were filled, and he gave them 'Napoleon.' Some considerable surprise and demur were exhibited. 'Doubtless, gentlemen,' said the proposer of the toast, 'you are somewhat astonished at the toast I have given you. But, as authors, I feel that the name of Napoleon should be held in honour, and accorded the gratitude of remembrance; for let us never forget that he once shot a publisher!' The toast was drunk with enthusiasm.

A good subject for an article was suggested by Lord Houghton—'The misrepresented characters of Shakespeare.' It opens a wide and interesting field. He placed at the head of the list the Queen in *Hamlet*. 'Surely,' he said, 'it is abominable to see the way she is misrepresented on the stage. Stage tradition has no worse example. I picture the Queen in *Hamlet* as a handsome, well-got-up, fascinating woman—the "fast" woman of her time, in fact, beautiful, charming, and attractive; the sort of woman to make you say, "Well, upon my word, there's a good deal to be said for Claudius after all!" Instead of which, she is usually represented as a most respectable monthly nurse!'*

I like to remember that I have had the pleasure and honour of acting in three scenes with Lady Martin (Helen Faucit). Acting, however, is perhaps scarcely the right word for me to use in connection with my part of the work, for the little performance took place in her drawing-room, at a large evening 'At Home.' There was no stage. We just walked in at the door amongst the people who sat all round the room. I recollect, too, I was the more 'nervous' as I had been giving a recital that same evening in the suburbs, and did not get to Lady Martin's till the very last moment. It is physically impossible to me to act with any sense of ease and unself-consciousness under such circumstances. I watched Lady Martin with astonishment and admiration. For with her the room at once became a stage, and she acted with all the grace, finish, and conviction of the accomplished actress treading the boards.

* Since then the character has been presented on the stage after Lord Houghton's picture. It was thus acted by Miss Leighton at the Princess's, in Mr. Wilson Barrett's production of *Hamlet*, and was a most effective performance.

We did two scenes from the *School for Scandal*, and the balcony scene from *Romeo and Juliet*. Thus it will be seen that my parts afforded as wide a field for the delineation of varieties of age as of manners. It was, however, unimportant who was the old Sir Peter, or the young Montague, for every one's attention was naturally given to the Lady Teazle and to the Juliet.

I wished I could be merely auditor and spectator. Being performer and speaker, criticism was impossible to me. But it seemed to me that Lady Martin's performance of Sheridan's charming heroine was very fine. She has the 'style' which is necessary for the part. For I have always held that Lady Teazle should have 'style' even perhaps to slight exaggeration. The fine ladyism would perhaps be a little overdone by the clever country girl who is so bitten with fashionable life, and has adopted with delight all the manners and tricks, all the pass-words and extravagances, of society. She would guard herself at every turn, and accentuate the airs and graces she copies. It is often said that great manners are a thing of the past in society. If so, it is small wonder they should not often be seen on our stage.

When one sees an actress like Lady Martin, one realizes what a loss this is; for then one is taught how high spirits can, though unrestrained, be perfectly graceful: and naturalness, even when daringly true to life, may be idealized and refined. The sight is a good one, and has its lesson; for nowadays, alas! high spirits on the stage are generally more than a little boisterous, and naturalness strikes such a low average that it often sinks to commonplace.

Lady Martin was most kind to me; as she always has been, from my first start in my profession. I shall always remember with pleasure that I can actually say that I have acted with Helen Faucit.

I saw her once on the stage. It was at Drury Lane, shortly before my father's death—about 1867, I think. She played Imogen in *Cymbeline*. It lives in my memory as a splendid performance, at once refined and powerful.

I have had few kinder friends in all my career than the late Lady Combermere. Her name occurs often in my note-books, in record of pleasant parties and hospitable feasts. At her table I met many interesting as well as distinguished people. She was herself a remarkable woman. Her vitality, her memory, and sharp humour; her love for certain phases of art, and her capability in a sense as an artist herself; her general cleverness, and her interest in life and the world, were astonishing. These things in her possessed a perennial youth, but it was a youth that preserved itself and its scheme of living intact. It did not advance with the time. It wore the dress and had the manners of 'the early Victorian period.' That was what made the whole thing unique. It was at once essentially old-fashioned and yet not in the very least old. It was rather younger than much that is quite modern.

What, too, was more extraordinary in its way in London than her house in Belgrave Square? It was a bit of history in the way of decorative art. I was told, when first I knew her, that she would soon cease to care for or to notice me; that her interest in me would simply be the old and often-told (too often-told, I think) story of the great world and an artist. But it was not so. There was no touch of it in all our intercourse. Unfailing and generous kindness, unflagging interest and courtesy, something I am proud to call affection, marked the friendship that, beginning with my earliest attempts in my profession, and following its career with always increasing sympathy, lasted through many years, and leaves me a memory that must always be bright.

One of the last autograph letters I had from her accompanied a handsome clock which she sent to me—one of her many gifts. The note seemed to me a model of happily turned courtesy.

'48, Belgrave Square.

'Dear Mr. Clifford Harrison,
 'Pray accept the means of recording the passage of time till we meet, which will be, I am sure, more rapid for you than for
  'Yours always sincerely,
   'M. Combermere.'

A house well known both socially and artistically in London was Cromwell House. Lady Freake (now the Dowager Lady Freake) had a gift for organizing parties and entertainments there of exceptional interest. Of all these perhaps the most notable were the Waverley tableaux—tableaux from the Waverley novels, arranged by well-known artists.

There were two nights of the tableaux : six or seven novels being represented each night. And this double set was given three times. A large sum was made, I believe, for the charities concerned. All the world and his wife, his sisters, his cousins, and his aunts, flocked to see the sight. Seats were engaged by cablegram from U.S.A. Royalty was present and expressed approval. Great folks applauded, and smaller folk crowded to look at the double tableaux of the stage and the audience. For often not the least remarkable tableaux were to be seen in the unconscious grouping of the guests assembled. It must have been a difficult matter to arrange it all, and keep everything going smoothly and pleasantly. But Lady Freake is an adept at work of that kind. And the whole performance—the whole performances, I may say, for there were six—gained a perfect success.

Millais, I think, took *The Heart of Midlothian;* Leslie, *Woodstock;* Marcus Stone, *Kenilworth;* Sant, *The Abbot;* Lady Butler, *Rob Roy*, etc. All the pretty women and all the smart young men of London were gathered together for the heroes and heroines. One regretted there was not to be a series of

tableaux from Tennyson's *Dream of Fair Women*. The dream might have been realized.
I read the extracts from the novels which described each tableau. It was impossible to give them with much dramatic effect. It was a sort of compromise between reciting and reading. I had to speak very loudly, for the darkness and my position—close to the proscenium—made it difficult to make one's self heard. I read as quietly as might be under the circumstances but the circumstances were such as developed in me, to my mind, an irresistible likeness to a showman.

On another occasion there were tableaux representing Schiller's *Song of the Bell*.

I am not good at figures when they run high. I could scarcely, therefore, reckon rightly the number of times I have recited for Lady Freake at Cromwell House, and at Twickenham, or the kindnesses I have received at her hands. The sum-total, however, is an imposing one, and is chronicled very truly and deeply in my grateful remembrance.

I have often been accused by those who know me best of indulging tediously in reminiscence and retrospection. Memory, with capital *M*, it is stated, is my favourite word

I think that I must plead guilty to this. Therefore I give myself credit for rejecting many pages in my note-books which I am sorely tempted to put in this section. Yet I hope I shall be pardoned for taking one of such pages, because I feel that such thoughts are indeed a part of my life (and sometimes I think the larger part), and claimed their portion even of my busiest days.

I had no better pleasure than to go to a place where I was due for a recital in time to wander about, and do a little sketching, and forget for the nonce why I had come to the place. Pleasant afternoons before my work in the evening, and pleasant evenings after my work in the afternoon, thus find record in my note-books—hours of most refreshing leisure and dreaming, spent in exploring unknown places or revisiting those well known. The passage I quote describes such an afternoon at Deal one day in June.

. . . I arrived here (Deal) early in the morning, went to the little hotel on the beach, wandered about, and sentimentalized to my heart's content. For why? Deal has much of sentiment to tell me of, and is fraught with recollections of childhood. It sings a song to me that begins with the simple but potent words of Hood's poem—

'I remember, I remember,'

It was at Deal that I got my first sight of the sea. How well I recollected it all as I walked about the old town! Many of the remembered scenes are a good deal altered, of course, but much remains.

In the long ago to which my memory looked I used to stay at an ivy-covered cottage with a neat, bright garden in front, and a boat-building yard opposite. I was allowed to poke about the yard, and in the long wooden shed where the men worked. Everywhere there was a delightful litter of rudders, and masts, and ropes, and old iron, and shavings, and sawdust—all the paraphernalia of fishing-boats and a carpenter's shop. The place 'smelt good' of resinous wood and tar. I went to look at the little narrow straggling street that led up from the cottage on to the beach. There was a capstan and a big fishing-boat to be seen at the end of the street, just as of old, beautifully outlined against the sky. I remembered the delighted run up to the beach the first morning I was there, and the awed pause as I stood under the nets that were festooned from boat to boat, and got my first sight of the sea. Long summer afternoons came to my mind, when my brother Frank and I would be for hours searching for shells, paddling about in the waves, or half burying ourselves in shingle. Then there were the sandhills beyond Sandown—a region mountainous and eventful, all of beautiful sand dotted with tall flowering sea-grasses, and covered here and there with dainty pink convolvuluses and pale horned poppies. The dykes were full of water-flowers and cresses; and beyond them lay rich meadow-lands mile after mile, where cattle trooped and cropped the grass. Ruskin, with his perfect feeling for all that is beautiful in Nature, mentions somewhere the extraordinary charm of a beach or line of sandhills seen from the land side, rising up against the sky, and when the sea itself is out of sight. The passage always recalls exquisite memories of that time of early boyhood at Deal to me, when I often realized this effect. Sandown Castle is now almost swept away by the sea. When the waves once broke into it, they wrought a swifter destruction than any siege of man. But my early recollection of it s as a picturesque ruin where you could still trace and explore the dungeons and oubliettes, and play at being knights of

> 'Old, far off, unhappy times,
> And battles long ago.'

There we extemporized dramas of the Iron Age amongst the battlements. The portcullis and drawbridge still remained; the moat and foss were there to quicken imagination and suggest agreeable incidents of calamity and woe. The moat was fast silting up with sea-sand, and there were delicate shells and star-fish in the dungeons. But this only added something of faerie to romance, and enabled us to mix up the drama of *The Tempest* with that of *Richard III*.

Deal is rich in castles and in windmills; and what things can be more suggestive and picturesque? At Kingsdown the chalk cliffs run high, and grow all sorts of flowers, and present all kinds of thrilling opportunities for the development of adventure and of vertigo. Smuggling stories abound. The Goodwins, with their line of surf by day, and the warning stars of their light-ships at night, are a point of perpetual interest. It seems to me that an old boatman, who was a great friend of mine, used to tell me a new and amazing story of the sea every day, and I have no doubt they were all quite true. Ah! it was delightful, wonderful! a time of romance and beauty! And at Deal! Why not? The world is all Fairyland if we see it so. Deal makes a very respectable Fairyland. And wandering about there this afternoon, I caught a glimpse of it here and there; for I am glad to say the ivory gates are not quite shut even yet. Indeed, there are times when I think they open wider and wider. . . .

Afternoons and evenings of this sort have made up the pleasantest part of many busy days, and sometimes they found expression in my sketch-books more than in my notes. Anyway, they were generally dedicated to that Memory with a capital *M* to which I have referred. And if it be true that this word and the world it represents is so great a power to me and offers to my feet so inviting a field for a mild form of mental aberration, let me own that it is a bright world to me, thanks to the atmosphere that affection and friendship have given to it. Dark shadows and bitter spots of regret it has, and not without pathos are even its brightest walks; and yet, in ending these notes of reminiscence, I recall Renan's beautiful simile of memory to the pealing of the lost bells of the fabled city of Ys, and can truly say with him that I too love ' at times to pause and listen to those gentle vibrations:' and that, whenever and howsoever their ghostly voices rise on my ears, I can answer—

> ' Ring on your heart-made music,
> Ring, blessed bells of Ys.'

III.
NOTES OF OBSERVATION.

'Mr. Wegg was an observant person; or, as he himself put it, he "took a powerful sight o' notice."'—DICKENS, *Our Mutual Friend.*

III.

Clovelly, 1888—Lucas Malet—Third-class passengers—The fen country — Miracle—Experience—Pleasant visits—Lady Ruthven—Memorable whispers—Edinburgh—Sir Noel Paton—Mrs. Dunbar—*Vathec*—Ghosts—Hamilton Palace—An Echo-temple—Contrasts—A minuet—A professionalism—*Venice Preserved* in the Midlands—Wagner—'Ideal' art—Realistic art—Turner's pictures—National type of face—A new reciter—At the Royal Academy—Memorable sermons—Rhythmic reading—Reading the Church Service—Mr. Gladstone's reading—Personal characteristics to be preserved—Scholastic elocution — Can it be taught?—Stage declamation—The French *e* in declamation.

It is the holiday season (August, 1888). The voice of the tourist is heard in the land, and, alas! it is a voice that, for certain days at this time of the year, actually resounds at Clovelly. As far as possible the undesired and uninvited popularity is deprecated. The 'tripper' is given scant welcome and scantier accommodation.

He finds no restaurant or tea-garden. The two inns seem to grudge him the *table d'hôte* which is provided for the regular and respected visitor. A few of the cottages announced that the tripper may therein find 'hot water.' But in what form it is to be applied to him might sometimes admit of question. But welcome he can do without, for he makes himself at home wherever he goes; and refreshment he needs not, for he brings it with him. The paper that covered it and the bottle that held it are left behind as legacies. The few flowers and rarer ferns which are left in the woods and lanes are taken away by him as trophies. He comes by coach, he comes by wagonette, he comes most of all by steamer. If he comes by the latter, he is often unwell when he lands, and is scarcely recovered when the bell rings to summon him aboard again. I have seen him arrive on a rough day, and be landed in a small boat (as all visitors by sea to Clovelly must be)—a boat which ships water plentifully at every wave. I have watched him from the pier—in common with a line of delighted and anticipating fishermen and coast-guardsmen—put on his tall hat and overcoat, and prepare to 'walk the plank' from the head of the rocking boat to a seaweed-covered boulder. Pale, and doubled up with terror, he has clutched the shoulders of the boatman who stood knee-deep in the water to hold the boat; he has launched himself thus on the slippery plank, slid at once easily all along it, and arrived on shore seated firmly in the surf—to the cheers of the onlookers. He suffers a good deal sometimes on these voyages. He seldom seems to really care for the place. 'This is a comical sort of a place,' is his usual criticism. 'I suppose we shall come to the shops presently,' a large lady in front of me remarked one day, toiling hotly up the village, with eyes on the rough cobbled steps up which she laboured. When she got to the high-road at the top, she looked round with a sigh of relief, and asked me if I could show her the way to Clovelly. She had passed right through it. I was wicked enough to direct her and her party up to the Bideford road and turn to the right. They are probably still walking on toward the Land's End.

Every year, I suppose, throughout the land, the 'tripper' appears with increased energy. His name is legion; his manners are *nil*. He is the child of the century. He is one of the undeveloped growths of Modernity, and form: part of the new order to which the old is everywhere yielding. The new order may justify him in time, and evolve unsuspected beauty and intelligence out of him. But a present he is immature, and can only be looked on as representing the first stage of an emancipation and of a demonocratic joy which as yet is a little burdensome and boisterous. For he has the spirits of childhood without its graces. He jumps on the toes of the parent civilization. But there he is—where, in fact, is he not?—and Clovelly, for its part, must make the best of him.

But it is hard work to do this. For probably there are few places of its size, or rather of its smallness, which could show daily so large an army of sight-seers as Clovelly. The place has a unique reputation.

I think it was Goëthe who said that wherever a man does anything supremely well, the whole world enters into a conspiracy that he shall never do it again. There is something of the kind to be said about places. When a place has been pronounced unusually beautiful everybody goes thither to see it, and, as far as may be, to prevent anybody of taste and sober judgment repeating the statement. Byron, for example, sings of

'Clarens! sweet Clarens, birthplace of deep love."

So all the world and his wife trot off to sweet Clarens. Steamers and railways and tramcars are started to take the world and his wife hither. Hotels, pensions, and villas are built and run up to entertain them. Shops and restaurants cluster thickly to supply their wants. Money-box-like churches and chapels show that the world and his wife are church-goers, and enable them to have a little harmless amusement in organizing bazaars and concerts to pay off the debts on those buildings. Telegraph wires, electric-light wires, and telephone wires weave a scratch-cradle all along the shore, and 'sweet Clarens, birthplace of deep love,' is made 'up to date' for the comfort and well-being of the world and his wife. Only one day it occurs to somebody to say, ' But, dear me! I don't think all this is very pretty; what could Bryon have been thinking about?' And then the sad fact is discovered that the world and his wife have been and spoilt sweet Clarens, and that it is not likely to be the birthplace of any deep love again.

Such a fate, however, seems far, happily from beautiful Clovelly. In spite of popularity and all its dangers, the place remains wonderfully primitive and simple. Fortunately, the property is in the hands of a lady who is no minded to have it spoilt, if good taste and truth of living can keep it as it is. No hideous lodging-houses are built, nor smart hotel. The temptation must be great and urgent to give way to public demand. But if it be, it is nobly resisted; and Clovelly remains, more or less the fishing-village of Kingsley's pages and of Hook's pictures. And when the summer visitors are gone, it forgets that it is a professional beauty, and goes its ways, and faces real life, and renews its youth. It seems scarcely possible that in the nature of things this can go on very long. But we must be grateful that it has held good all these years. As old cottages decay, of course larger ones will appear, typifying the thin end of the wedge. It is the fate of all such places, sooner or later to change their mood. It can scarcely be otherwise in these days.

Clovelly is something like a little Swiss mountain village in its construction, though is so essentially Devonian in its features

But it has one feature that makes it even more poetic to my mind than any Swiss village I have ever seen. The presence of 'the misty and mournful Atlantic,' out beyond Lundy, gives a touch that is grander both in human and in natural drama than the snows of Savoie and Valais, or the white wonder of Bernese Oberland.

The beauty of Covelly street is well known. It has been described a hundred times, painted and drawn a thousand times, and photographed —well, I can never count beyond millions! But I do not think it has ever been thoroughly represented either by pen, pencil, or lens. Something of the charm is lost. The effect of drama, so distinct and strong, is either lowered into commonplace prettiness or accentuated into melodrama. The richness of the beauty is hard to give without exaggeration, and exaggeration destroys its other characteristic— reality. In the falsifying statements of the ordinary photograph, the angle of the ascent is always flattened, the height of the wooded cliff is understated, and the stairway of the street is therefore not sufficiently steep. Out of some fifty photographs of Clovelly street which I possess, not more than half a dozen are true.

In painting, the artist has the difficulty of dealing with whitewashed cottages and walls. Whitewash is hard and glaring; yet when once you seize the fact that it is also a characteristic of the country, and that Clovelly without its whitewash would also be without the romance and feature of North Devon, you get to like it, and find that it possesses, like most realities, a something more valuable in the landscape than mere prettiness. Most of the drawings and paintings of Clovelly seize its letter, but not its spirit, and degenerate into 'studies' of some rather theatrical-looking cottages. The cottages offer the possibility of this aspect, if looked at with a too conventional 'artistic' eye. Some of them are made of red cob, and have woodwork about them; some are thatched and dormer windowed; some are broken into archways over the climbing road, and built partly into and out of the hillside; and some are perched on all sorts of coigns of flower-grown and orchard-shadowed rock. And all are bright with nasturtiums and geraniums, with bushes of hydrangea and veronica, whilst fuschias grow as high as the doorways, and arch overhead with boughs of crimson blossom. It is difficult to depict su-

incidents and preserve any height of dignity and drama. Yet the charm of Clovelly exists in this combination. Thus, I suppose, it is that very few of the pictures we see of Clovelly do it justice.

The many curves and incidents of the steep staircase which is called Clovelly street, are each a perfect natural picture, yet a picture which oftentimes art cannot reproduce, because the artist can find no technical point of view. Surprising combinations of things occur — things far removed alike in intention and distance, brought into juxtaposition by the sharpness of the ascent and descent. Thus you get glimpses of the parapet of the climbing street high up above the houses; the old sailors sitting by the flagstaff at the 'Look-out' appear to be on the tops of the trees; the cottages and gardens at Mount Pleasant seem to have their foundations on the roof of the New Inn. Looking downward, the rosy faces of children coming up the street are outlined against the blue waters of the bay. Over the chimneys of the cottages in the next zigzag of the road, and under the trellised fuchsias at the door of a cottage on this, small vignetted pictures are seen of the quay-pool, with the fishing-boats at anchor, and the nets hung up to dry on the sickle-shaped stone pier. The donkeys, bringing panniers of coal up from the brig unlading in the little harbour, come up through an archway at a point where the road seems to drop sheer on to the beach, amongst some children playing in an old boat. Through boughs of apple-trees, thickset with red and green and amber fruit, you see the white surf breaking along the circling shore two miles away.

But all this part of Clovelly is well known. Well known, too, is the Hobby, Gallantry Bower, and the Wilderness. These are the chief and most celebrated features of Clovelly. But there are other features, less known, but scarcely less beautiful, although the beauty may be of a less popular and obvious type.

In the nooks and corners of the deer-park, for instance, there are scenes that suggest the possible presence of Rosalind and Orlando, and woods which have a delicious sense of remoteness, and retain, undoubtedly, a secret knowledge of Elfland and the whereabouts of Oberon.

And, still better, on the long summer days, when Clovelly is amusing its light moments by pretending to be a tea-garden, and even the park is trodden of many feet—for the hand that holds the gates is too kind to keep them locked—there is a delectable No-man's land, called the 'Up Country,' which will be found to be solitary enough, and full of character of a commendably unpopular kind. It lies up above Hagglepit and Buddlemoor, beyond the coach road to the left as you drive to Bude. It is a little like the Border in Northumberland. Here the modern painter would find subjects to his heart's content. There is no touch of the soft beauty and dangerous decorativeness of Clovelly street; no touch even of the arcadian and sylvan spirit of Clovelly Park. It is all bleak and grand, and full of suggestions fitted to a country which faces the open Atlantic, and leads on to the region of Arthuric romance. It is a tableland of open, windswept country, very rough and very poor—as the parson will know to his cost, a good deal of it being glebe land.

You look out over miles of low, scrubby, undulating country, intersected with bog and ragged baulks, and dotted here and there with lonely outlying farms. In the foreground there are patches of yellow gorse. They are very beautiful in spring, and load the air with rich aromatic smell. Great tufts of coarse grass, banks full of wild flowers, and ditches with masses of forget-me-nots, are the chief features of the barren fields. Long lines of stunted beeches and dwarf oaks, whipped westward by the Atlantic gales, stretch away inland, and give everywhere a heavy, sombre colour to the scene. To the right, the country sweeps on into Cornwall and to Bursden Moor, over which Amyas Leigh and Will Carey rode in hot haste to Moreland Mouth on the Queen's service. And far ahead, beyond Holdsworthy, thirty miles off, you see the ridge of Dartmoor against the sky, generally in a haze of faint, pale, tremulous blue. The place is very lonely. One fancies it must have looked much the same for hundreds of years. The few cottages, slated and whitewashed, which cluster here and there in the less exposed places, look rather alarmed and apprehensive, as if they liked to keep close and cling hard to the ground, knowing that when the western sea wakes up and the wind sweeps in, elevation is dangerous. The sea of Bideford Bay is forgotten, hidden away behind the rising country to the north. Often there is no sea at all in sight. But if ever, between a V-shaped opening out there to the west, you catch the blue-grey line of the sea, you know that it is the open ocean you are looking at, and that that mysterious voice which comes up across the land, deep, distant, arousing, continuous, is the voice of the Atlantic swell breaking in thunder on the rocks of Hartland, six miles away. To one who has an ineradicable distrust of Nature, and a rooted dislike of all 'violent exhibitions of the elemental energies,' this country would be terrible in wind and weather. The possibilities of the place seem tremendous. One does not need to be told that, looking westward, you face three thousand miles of open sea, straight away to Labrador, or that the coast-line is one of the deadliest in our island; you seem to know it all by instinct. It is written in clear characters everywhere. Yet, seeing it all for the first time in the calm of a grey August afternoon, when Nature seemed asleep, and the sea was like a dense grey floor under a quiet sky of opal cloud, it seemed to me as tender and beautiful as it was poetic.

The long drive from Bideford to Clovelly is thought to be very dull. Certainly, in so far as it is a long drive to or from a station which is the beginning or end of a very much longer journey, it is dull, not to say tiresome and tedious. But in itself, simply judged by the country through which the road passes, I cannot think it at all dull. It possesses too strong a character for that. When people tell me such and such a country is dull, I book it directly as a place to go to with my sketch-book. I shall probably find it an excellent and suggestive field for work. The dull places to me are the 'pretty pretty' places. A country with any strong individuality is always picturesque. To an artist going to Clovelly, I should recommend this very road from Bideford, the 'Up Country,' Hartland, and Wrinklebury. Then, too, this road from Bideford gives a certain dignity to Clovelly, which it would lose were it easier of access. The fact that Clovelly lies where it does, a sort of oasis of beauty in the sterile and stern country all round it, raises the value of its beauty in a very remarkable manner, and preserves it from the touch of the theatrical prettiness it might otherwise have to own to.

Seen in its summer dress, bright with sunshine and flowers on fine days, and bright even on wet ones with the permeated light and illuminated shadows of summer-time, Clovelly seems to be a gay, smiling, glad place. It has that mood. But, like all places—and shall we not say people also?—that can laugh and sing when things go well and light is full, Clovelly can be mournful enough when the light is low and things go wrong, or, at least, go heavily. It has a power of sadness as it has of joy. In fact, it is curiously foreign, as has been often said. An old coast-guardsman there, who likes to prophecy the weather, always 'hedges' very discreetly on his forecasts, and says, 'But then, you see, sir, what makes for fine makes for wet, and vicey worser.' It is as true as it is tiresome. And what makes for beauty and gladness in a scene makes also, under other conditions, for grimness and gloom. Italy basks and laughs in the sunshine, and dwindles and shivers and sulks in the rain. The great snow-mountains are fairy palaces when the world is bright, and sheeted ghosts when the brightness passes away. Clovelly loves the sunshine—it seems made for it; but in depression it strikes a deep note. When the winter shadows are dark and dense, and the winter colouring is heavy and sombre; when the sun gets low in its circuit through the sky, and the light at the best but slants across the village and touches the place here and there with a glow as of some summer evening, Clovelly grows strangely sad. To watch the herring-boats and trawlers go out then, when the wind is rising, and there is a moan in the sea all round the coast, seems very far off any experience of the bright August days when the men are away on summer voyages, till the winter fishing begins, and the village has trimmed itself up to earn an honest penny by the visitors who come crowding to the place. Nay, some of those who know Clovelly best say that there is always in it, to them, an underlying sense of possible drama and sadness. The tombstones in the churchyard which bear the words, 'Drowned at sea,' have a record also in the hearts of the people. One fancies that the Clovelly folk have got the wonderful clear blue of their eyes from looking, generation after generation, at sea and sky. Perhaps the sea and sky have coloured their lives as well—not only with the gladness of the summer days, but also with the long rigour of the winter nights and the knowlege of the storm. Nearly every cottage has a tale which compels the tears of those who tell it. The romance of the place is deep and true. It is no mere gloss or picture; it is a fact.

I find, in some of my brother's letters, passages that present Clovelly under a different aspect to that known to the visitor. One of these passages I will quote.

'... Just as we were going to evening church, we heard there was a large steamer—the *Uppisham*, of Cardiff, three thousand tons—ashore at Hartland, and that the coastguard and a number of fishermen had gone off with the rocket apparatus to see if they could be of service. They were soon on the spot. The vessel was in a bad way. She was on the rocks, great iron ridges that lie like rows of gigantic shark's teeth, facing the west, and no power it seemed could save her. The sea was pouring over her. The night was fast closing in. The only way to get at her was over the face of the cliffs, a matter of about four hundred feet, pretty straight down. "You can't go over there, sir; that's impossible." "Can you show us a better way, my lad?" "No, sir." "Then that's our way." So the scaling-ladder was thrown over and fixed, and down they went, chief officer and men and rocket apparatus, as best they could, in the wild wind and gloom. The scaling-ladder only reached sixty feet. They found a place to stand on, a mere shelf, somewhere in the cliff. They hauled down the ladder, and fixed it there again. Then down once more. Refixed it; and so on, till somehow they reached the bottom. There was a furious sea and blinding surf. The first rocket missed, through the force of the wind; the second caught in the rigging, where the men on board could not reach the rope; the third fell clean across the deck. Meanwhile, the first mate, in despair, thinking their efforts had failed (there was some inevitable delay in firing the rockets), had tried to reach the shore and affect a communication by wading to them on the rocks from the vessel. Poor fellow! of course he was struck down and swept away, and never seen again. The first person to come ashore was one of the officers. "There's a lady on board, sir; the cap'n's wife." "Then what are *you* doing here?" our chief officer shouted. "Get out of my sight; women come first." They were all saved, seven persons. The rest, eighteen seamen, had taken to the boats and gone off round the point.

'Meanwhile I was conducting the service

with a very scanty congregation, for Clovelly was naturally all astir, having launched the lifeboat in search of the two boats that had gone off from the vessel, and every one was assisting. It is difficult to read prayers and preach a sermon when an Atlantic gale is blowing. You hear the wind gather and rush and roar over hill and dale, till it strikes the church full, and then goes thundering and battering and bellowing round the walls, and making all the windows dance and rattle, and tearing at the doors, and drowning every sound within, till you might fancy all the air was full of malign spirits struggling and straining and clamouring there outside for entry into the house of prayer. The physical exertion of speaking under such circumstances is considerable, to say nothing of the effect on the nerves, with the sense of what may be going on in the bay in that wild tumult of the winds and waves. We sang the hymn, *Eternal Father, strong to save*, and I asked for the prayers of the faithful few "for those in peril on the sea," an appeal that has a very potent meaning in Clovelly Church. At last the Benediction was said, and the service was over.

'I ran down into the village. The lifeboat

was just in. They had seen nothing of the boats that had left the steamer. But at midnight a man at the end of the pier caught sight of a boat within a few yards of him. "Here they come!" Would they get in, or be swamped in the breakers? They were nearly exhausted when the boat at last was beached. There were thirteen of them. They had been eight or nine hours in the most terrific sea. How they got round the point, how they kept afloat, no one could tell. Their little boat was so rotten you could pick the wood to pieces with your thumb. A quarter of an hour more and they would have sunk. When they got in they were close down to the water, and all the seams of the boat were giving. Just in time they saw the light on the pier. They were carried up to the warm kitchen of the Red Lion. They had lost everything, and were entirely dependent on the kindness of our people. Every one was ready to help them. The second boat was cast up the next morning at Braunton. One man, a Swede, was saved; the other four had been washed out of her and drowned.

'Next day I made arrangements for getting the thirteen men home, some to London, others to Cardiff, others to Liverpool. The Shipwrecked Mariners' Society—for which I am honorary agent here—is a generous friend to seafaring folk.

'Truly there is "sorrow on the sea." But there is courage, and "love strong as death" likewise. These men told me how they wanted the captain's wife to come with them, and how she refused to do so, and took her stand on the bridge by the side of the "cap'n" when they pushed off, whilst the waves poured over the vessel, and every one felt sure that all on board the steamer would never live to see another day or get to land. The preventive men gained great credit for their plucky conduct, which they greatly deserved. For it is no joke to go down a cliff of four hundred feet on a scaling-ladder, in a gale, at six o'clock in a November evening, and get yourself and your rockets landed at the bottom. Their services were handsomely rewarded by the Board of Trade. As the shipwrecked men drove off to the station, on their way home, on Tuesday morning, they gave hearty cheers for the " Coastguard " and " Clovelly." '

I believe it is now an open secret amongst

all reading people that 'Lucas Malet' is the *nom de plume* under which Mrs. William Harrison, youngest daughter of Charles Kingsley, writes. She has dedicated one of her novels—*A Counsel of Perfection*—to me, as her brother-in-law. Therefore there is no literary indiscretion in my speaking of the relationship. And, indeed, not to do so would but ill represent the source from which this book is taken, or myself the writer; for in my note-books there are many pages about her, and many letters from her. We are, too, I am proud to say, such very dear friends that I could scarcely omit to name her in these notes. Without venturing, or wishing, to intrude domestic and family life in any way into publication, I may permit myself to say that some of the brightest and happiest pages in my note-books are those which record my visits to my brother's rectory at Wormleighton and at Clovelly, and his and my sister-in-law's visits to me in London; and, further, to regret in one sense, that those pages cannot find place here.

Criticism of any kind of her work is as impossible from me as is description of any personal nature. And, after all, what must be of best interest is, if possible, to give words of her own. She has given me permission to quote extracts from some of her letters. And that will be better than anything I can say. I must take the passages as they come in the letters I have preserved in my note-books, beginning with one dated 1880 at Lausanne.

'Lausanne, 1880.

'... He struck me, like so many great geniuses—don't be horrified; this is my pet and last theory, and works beautifully—as being merely a *pipe* through which divine music is poured into the world. *He* is nothing as far as human life goes; he is a mere vehicle, instrument, for the revelation of higher powers. Shelley was such; many more great writers, poets, musicians, painters. We have no right to quarrel with their vices or criticize their lives. They are not to be expected to conform to our social laws; we must take what they give us thankfully, and leave the rest. Only let us never marry, live with, or be related to them, unless we are cut out for saints and martyrs. . . .

* * * * *

'As to Rubenstein's playing, it is so amazing

that you cease to be amazed. In serious, tender, or grand music it is perfect, wonderful, beyond description lovely; but, alas! alas! he played a valse, and notably a galop, and his gymnastics on the piano are comic. . . . I should suppose he has no humour, and not the slightest conception of what *appearances* mean, and so, alas! the ridiculous treads hard on the heels of the sublime, the music degenerates into noise, and the man into the semblance of a fighting bear more than anything else I can think of. Humour bothers me. It certainly prevents the *very* spiritual developments of our nature; gets horribly in the way of great preachers, poets, and saints, etc.; and yet without it a man is always liable to—in plain words—make a fool of himself. . . .'

'Wormleighton Vicarage, Leamington,
'March 19, 1883.

'. . . Your remarks on the love of dullness among our countrymen specially pleased me. It is very true that English people distrust everything in every department that does not carry ballast in the shape of obvious dullness. The Teuton loves to be dull—doesn't feel safe unless he is dull. I fancy it is just our dullness which makes us incapable of satisfying Celtic Ireland. I am Irish enough myself to know that I should soon grow ripe for any quantity of crimes under the rule of a number of . . . , and they very fairly represent the average Englishman, you know.

'. . . Need I tell you that I was greatly pleased about the *Alkestis*.* I thought it was a great venture, and did not, I confess, at all expect that it would please. I have an idea— which may, of course, be pure imagination, because it is not easy to criticize one's self—that all that I attempt to say, and certainly all that I feel, is too cool and clear to be very interesting. People, both in poetry and prose, like a *warm muddle*, which excites them with indefinite suggestions, and which is considered valuable and subtle in proportion as it is confused and incomprehensible. That notion that everybody's thought is too great for words as they are, and that consequently they must coin new ones, or turn and distort their sentences out of all common form and grammar, so as to render their precious and profound meaning,— all this seems to me just so much affectation,

* *A Chorus from the Alkestis*, by Lucas Malet, unpublished, but which I recited at several of my public recitals.

and want of patience, and want of real culture. It is on the dull Teutonic side of things again. The Latin says what he wants to say clearly and trenchantly, and if he finds his thought too big for his words, he waits modestly till he has found words big enough to clothe it. Matthew Arnold is a perfect master in all this matter, and, as an author, how very far he is from popularity! It seems to me that Coleridge, Carlyle, and German philosophy have done the English language and English style an injury which it will take generations to get over.

'. . . The hard part of being clergy-people is that your conduct must be all of a piece—as far as you can make it so. In any of the other professions, you can do your business well and diligently, and then go off and sin mildly with a good conscience. But there is no respite—or should be none—from good deeds and words and irreproachable living in the clerical profession. The result is a lamentable mediocrity, for the struggle to maintain a condition of constant good behaviour exhausts all our stock of energy, and while one escapes being obviously indiscreet, I hope, one entirely fails to rise to any remarkable heights of saintship.

'This letter is only worthy of . . . in length, and dull enough to have been written by a pure and unadulterated Teuton. You needn't read it though!'

'Clovelly Rectory.

'. . . There is a good deal of sickness and some distress here. The sailors can't get berths, the shipping trade is so bad; and the farmers are giving nine shillings a week to the labourers, so that times are bad. Last night W——, having been down the village all the afternoon, went up to Dyke between eight and nine o'clock, pitch dark, and a north-easterly gale, to carry wraps of sorts to a woman who has been nearly dying, to keep her warm at all; all the wretched coverings had to be taken off the children's beds, and they had to sleep in their clothes the night before last, poor dears! I am afraid I am becoming a bitter radical, socialist, anything. It makes one rage to see people actually want fire, food, and clothes. I am thankful to say we are able to feed two or three people every day. At moments one's own food would choke one, I think, if one didn't do that. No doubt the giving is only a more refined form of selfishness, but it is a form, after all, which is of practical benefit to somebody else—which most of one's sins are not.

'... Of course it is all a matter of degree. All we of the "comfortable classes" have more comfort in many ways than we actually need. But the fine folks really do seem to have an excess of comfort. I don't see how it is to be justified. They present an absurdity to the intelligence. . . .

'I am reading Darwin with a great deal of interest. I never sat down to him seriously before. His reverence for life, and beautiful gentleness towards animals, is very delightful. I, of course, am charmed to think we all have come from one original egg, and that there is only a difference of degree, not of kind, between my intellect and emotions and the Tobe's.* I talk to W—— about it, but he is a born spiritualist, not naturalist. He is willing to wander into pantheism and give all living things a share of spirit, and to claim cousinship with Tobes and cats and dogs. But he can't quite swallow the purely natural point of view, and admit the cousinship through his own animality, instead of their spirituality. To me this endless fertility

* A pet bird.

and power of development in nature seems more hopeful, more consolatory, than anything else I know. If we begin with spirit and with morals, one seems to end in despair; everything is so hopelessly dark, mysterious, unsatisfactory, unprovable. But if you begin with the idea of a single cell containing *life* countless ages ago, and see where it has worked up to by now, one gets a glimpse of the possibility of everlasting progression. Anyway, *living* is tremendously interesting; and it doesn't really much matter how things turn out eventually if they will only go on interesting one. This seems a distracted, disorganized, subversive sort of letter. Please forgive me. . . .'

'September 30, 1884.

'I wish you could have been here yesterday, or the church was really lovely. We had an mmense quantity of belladonna lilies (pink) ind pink hydrangeas from Hartland, and these n tall earthenware crocks, with leaves of ampas grass and oak boughs, the crocks built ound with vegetables and fruits of all colours, ere really delicious. The nets draped well cross the chancel arch. We fastened them ack against the wall with masses of coloured seaweed on either side of the arch, and had a great string of herrings all down the middle, hanging against the yellow nets. That handsome boy . . . helped us all Saturday. In his blue jersey, with a foreground of fruits of the earth and pink lilies, and a background of herring-nets, he really was superb. He is silent, stupid, alternately statuesque and wonderfully agile; he smiles at one occasionally out of a sort of beautiful vacancy, and wears a silver ring three-quarters of an inch thick on his third finger. Now, is not that an attractive *ensemble?* The silence and stupidity greatly heighten the effect, you know. That is a refinement of criticism . . . would stare at, would she not?'

'. . . To do anything very well is admirable, is it not, even if it is to do something wrong? I believe stupidity is the only unpardonable sin, and I am afraid that the majority of people commit it; with which cheerful kindly, and encouraging sentiment, I will leave off. . . .'

'. . . We have had a gale for three day and nights—the prince of the powers of the ai (who, according to the Rabbins, is a very evi spirit indeed) literally let loose upon us.

remember nothing so bad since we first came here. Even I sign a declaration against nature, and begin to feel it is rather horrible. I have almost hated Clovelly these last few days. It is too gloomy and too dramatic for persons who, like ourselves, can supply both gloom and drama, quite unassisted by outside circumstances, at a very cheap rate.'

'. . . It is one of one's first duties in life to respect the little unreasonablenesses of people's imaginations. It has taken me a long time to arrive at this, because if anything is *so*, it seems to me marvellous that any one should continue to think it otherwise when the actual fact has been explained. But I have come to see that half the agonies of life come from a want of delicacy in dealing with the imaginations of others, from the shock that is given sometimes by that (dear) brutality, common sense, to imagination; and that we must no more— unless one wishes to put people to the torture— insist upon their thinking what really is than upon their only suffering from bodily pain, and not from nervous pain. . . .

'. . . I believe that the air at sunset is always a little malignant; why, I don't know, but practically it seems to be so. Perhaps one's bodily strength flags a little with the flagging day. I am sure there are many more mysterious correspondences between ourselves and nature than have been admitted hitherto, except by the old magic-mongers, who seem to me to have mixed great real natural laws up most strangely with rank and grotesque superstitions. One trusts that in time the two may get themselves somewhat disentangled, only that means more to learn, understand, make room for, reckon with. And, Heaven knows, we have too much knowledge for our own happiness' sake, almost for our own sanity, to reckon with already.

'. . . My reading just now consists of a series of sandwiches, so to speak, composed of alternate slices of Darwin's life and Fielding's *Tom Jones*. This sounds abominably robust. But Darwin is not nearly as robust as one would fancy. He was the most gracious, tender-hearted, modest, humble-minded, unaggressive of men. . . . *Tom Jones* is quite in another style. I suppose I ought to be shocked at it. But *realism* is the topmost apple on the topmost bough of modern culture, and if we are to admire it in a contemporary Frenchman, why not in a Georgian Englishman? Then, too, Fielding is the most good-tempered of writers, and a gentleman into the bargain ; so that even in his undesirable moments he has a certain distinction—and his style is admirable.

'I have been a little troubled lest my own book should become a trifle hysterical, lest we should sit shrieking at Agony Point after the manner of ———. *Tom Jones* is an excellent corrective to any such tendency, keeps one's sense of humour lively, and makes one "wear one's rue with a difference"—such a difference, that at times it ceases to look like rue at all, and becomes really, I think, a very fragrant and pretty little posy. I believe it is immensely important *what* one reads when one is writing. Each book requires quite a different atmosphere on one's own mind, and that atmosphere must be maintained by the company one keeps, to a certain extent, and by the books one reads. I don't mean books of reference, but of general reading. I believe a contrast is best, and so I have been stoking myself with Walter Scott, Sterne, and now Darwin and Fielding. Walt Whitman remains prince among poets, *Brooklyn Ferry* and one or two others, notably the one containing the refreshing statement that "the ugliness of human beings is now acceptable to me," being gone through pretty frequently.'

'... The bullfinch is a duck. He sings nearly all day. He is so very big we think he must be a Russian bullfinch; they are twice the size of English ones. Also he utterly refuses to wash, which is suggestive of a Russian origin. As yet we have not discovered his name. "The Monsignore" and Mrs. Finch admire him very much, and talk to him, but I don't think he ever condescends to answer. The Monsignore is in full song—fine to see, limited to hear.

'... Our party of honourable women was reinforced on Saturday by a callow Guardsman, and a young gentleman with great good nature and great pecuniary prospects, his friend. Well-bred boys of eighteen to twenty, with endless kindness of disposition, of practical ability, of intellectual apathy, and no conversation, are a delightful invention. I am not sure that clever people are not a ridiculous superfluity. I find none pleasanter or more diverting than simple, silly folk—granting breeding. You must have that, or simplicity and silliness become awkwardness and vulgarity.'

'... She belongs to an older and more

dignified generation—a generation which knew not Darwin, and regarded us not as human animals, but as very wonderful creatures indeed, for whom the whole universe was made, this material world to supply us with a temporary, and heaven with an eternal, resting-place. God Himself—if I can say so reverently—was regarded as a sort of adjunct to man. We were the centre of things; of course, therefore, our manners were grand. Why not? We had every reason to think well of ourselves.

'Now a very considerable change has come "o'er the spirit of the dream," and with ascidians and apes in the background, the grand manner seems a trifle inappropriate. Of course I don't mind it. On the whole I think it makes the majority of us more merciful, unselfish, tender-hearted, unegotistic. It has widened the horizon so gloriously. It has taken away all fear of man; perhaps it has taken away too much of the fear of God too. I don't know. I can worship a God whose mercy I believe to be over *all* His works, much more happily and readily than I can a God of Abraham, Isaac, or Jacob, or even a God of a certain Church, or of the elect. It seems to me we moderns have come into a very magnificent inheritance—an inheritance so magnificent that it more than balances the superficial charm, the vague unplaced hopes and enthusiasms, the rather unbased sentimentalisms of the last generation. I am inclined to sing *Te Deum* over the new world, the realistic, capable, and indeed I do, *do* believe tender-hearted world, I see growing up around me.

'Of course there are evils, dangers, bad tendencies in it all; but then, in all great intellectual and moral movements there are those. It is inevitable. On the whole the movement is for the freedom and happiness of the majority. We shall not get individual figures of such "weight and movement," but the average will be higher.'

'. . . I have been very much interested in what you tell me about your visit to ——'s picture-gallery. It confirms the impressions I had already—that the thing is wholly godless and debased, a shameful, shameless business altogether, and in the vilest taste! Excuse strong expressions, but this gratuitous defiling of life—which is a poor business at best, in any case, for most of us—seems to me hideously wicked. I don't say *diabolically* because I don't believe the devil would have anything to say to it. He "believes and trembles"—so the New Testament says—which is modest of him, anyway, and comes very near being devout into the bargain.

'PERUGIA.'

'... Ever since we came here I have been wishing for you. You would delight in this place. The stately, serious, walled city seated on its hill overlooking the valley of the Tiber and the Umbrian plain, a land of corn, and wine, and oil, and olive, ringed round by ranges of purple-blue Apennine. Yesterday evening, after a day's soft rain, toward sunset, the valley, looking across towards Assisi, was all the colours of a peacock's train—greens, purples, blues, rich warm browns, and all with a certain glimmering living light on them—I suppose from the silver of the olives—which was enchanting. The town is of an upness and downness, and overarchedness, and bewalled and betoweredness which would delight you. Coming to this solemn Lombard-Gothic architecture after the audacities and worldliness of Renaissance churches and palaces in Rome, is very refreshing. The buildings here look a bit fierce, but they don't wear that look of triumphant making the best of both worlds which the Roman ones wear But then, I dislike Rome down to the ground, and below the ground, to the floor of its lowest catacomb. And it is *not* beautiful, as a city, from the artistic point of view. The ruins look much best in Smith's Classic Dictionary; you can learn all about them there, and that without being poisoned by pestilential exhalations from a soil made of graves. Some of the piazzas are rather delightful, and St. Peter's is the most glorious monument of ecclesiastical impertinence conceivable. It has nothing to do with religion—don't suppose it—but a great deal to do with a supreme pontiff and a college of Cardinals. One reads both the strength and weakness of Catholicism there, written in very plain type. It is immensely interesting and rather sad. Vanity of vanity, all is vanity; and that honey-coloured mountain of a church, with its colossal, sprawling, trumpet-blowing angels, is among the vainest imaginations of man—so it seemed to me. You know there is much to say besides this. The harmony of colour within, from the marbles and precious stones and gildings, softened by the vast height and breadth, is superb. The size of it all, indeed, captivates one's imagination.

Except the sea and the Alps, it is the only thing which has ever impressed me as really big. Yes, one thing more—London, if you drive from the West End far up into the City. I suppose the Steppes, out by the Caspian, would give one an agreeable impression of size too. But then, unfortunately, you know I have not managed to see them for myself, *yet!* It strikes me this letter is conceived in rather an extensive spirit, but it is so pleasant to get the use of one's pen again.'

'. . . Switzerland seems sadly wanting in distinction after Italy. I would like to talk to you about all that. Of course Italy is the country to draw and paint. Everything makes a picture, and there is no overloading, no superfluous detail. Pictorially speaking, its style is wonderfully chaste and refined—so very civilized, so aristocratic. But the human drama is too exhausting. We were talking at Berne the other night, watching the Oberland mountains, uplifted white and impassive to high heaven, of the strange difference of sentiment between them and Vesuvius. One's feeling towards the last is all hot with human passion ; he is a creature to be loved and dreaded and appeased, in a sense played with, though he is terrible.

But, good heavens! who would ever say that of the Jungfrau or the Eiger? They are as cold and pure as dead saints; he very much more like an exceedingly alive sinner. I wish you could see Naples. It shocked me for the first twenty-four hours, I could hardly look at it. Then I bundled Puritanism out of the window, and, artistically speaking, never enjoyed anything so much. Its beauty is all jostled by grotesque suggestion. It is abominable to every sense, it gave me malarial fever, but it remains indescribably delicious all the same. I did not intend to run on like this. I have seen Italy only from a vulgar, hired, numbered cab; I have been inside nothing, churches, galleries, so on; no traveller ever saw less; and yet the five months have been quite a liberal education, almost worth all the money and suffering they have cost me, one way and another. I shall be afraid ever to go back. Still, I have seen some things which are quite, for the future, part of the furniture of my mind.'

With these extracts, then, I must try to content myself in this matter. Full content I could not have under less than consigning to myself the part of a Boswell to my brother and sister-in-law's joint Dr. Johnson, and for that I have neither skill nor permission. Yet Boswell himself could not have brought more heartfelt admiration to his task than I should bring to mine, did I accept it.

Not the least interesting part of my work was the opportunity given of seeing many places. For, although anything savouring of the nature of sight-seeing has always been irksome to me, I am intensely interested in breaking new ground, and wandering about a town or country-side for the first time. Everything has its price, however, and the price paid for this constant pleasure was often rather heavy in the matter of travelling. Railway journeys are not my ideal of travelling, and they were sometimes tiresome or fatiguing. Yet they had their advantages and amusements.

They afforded me at my busiest time my best opportunities for study in learning new recitations. My fellow-travellers, too, often gave me a good deal of interest. I soon discovered that it is far more entertaining to travel third class than first. But I have always been so hunted and hedged about with a perpetual fear of draughts and 'colds,' that to go in a third-class carriage was a form of indulgence I could rarely give myself. I can, however, most truthfully say that the pleasantest, the most amusing, and also the most cultivated fellow-travellers I have ever met have been in the third class. Thus I have met not only obvious soldiers and sailors, putative tinkers and tailors, and more than suggestive thieves, but also most undoubted ladies and gentlemen. And once I remember coming up in the third class from Birmingham, when I was much rewarded. For in the carriage were three persons who deeply interested me.

The first was a jovial-faced, elderly woman of a comfortable, but undetermined appearance. She was a combination of a Mother Superior, Ophelia, and the Queen outside a booth in a country fair. She wore a bonnet and cloak distinctly suggestive of a religious habit. She carried a bunch of weedy flowers, which were scattered about and around her in a way that recalled the fourth act of *Hamlet*. And her dress was a dusty velveteen, trimmed with bugles, and hung about with chains and ornaments which might well have once been parts of a stage-regalia. She had a talkative face. She longed to converse, but no one was responsive. At last she couldn't stand it any longer. She broke the silence, and, with wonderful archness of expression and manner, said, 'Nobody can guess where these flowers are going.' Nobody attempted or evinced the slightest desire, to do so. She therefore repeated the words, partly as statement and partly as challenge. An old lady of mild and domestic exterior took it up, and quietly asked where they *were* going. 'To Clerkenwell prison!' said Queen-Mother-Ophelia triumphantly. The old domestic lady gave a little surprised, distressed cry. Then followed a long story, whereby we learned the jovial-faced woman was matron of a 'refuge;' that she had been to see some of the children who were on a visit to a dear kind lady (here followed a detailed account of the said lady, her position, her means, her charities, with a short survey of the husband's life and death); how one of the children had sent the flowers (she held up the rent and ragged blossoms) to her mother, who was in Clerkenwell prison; how she—Queen-Mother-Ophelia—was going to take them; how other flowers (more shreds held up, 'Here's rue for you') were from the garden of a farm far away, where a young woman, now in the refuge, was brought up. 'They will be an appeal to her,' said the stage-matron. 'She will see in them the blossoms she plucked as a child.' They certainly looked sufficiently decayed for the part. When the train stopped, the excellent lady gathered up her theatrical robes, clattering with twiddling bugles and jet, under the cloak of the matron, clutched the few stalks of the flowers which besprinkled the floor, and said, 'Now for the Clerkenwell prison!' leaving us all impressed, in varying degrees, with the drama and truthfulness of her story.

But the most interesting people sat directly opposite me. It is difficult to describe them. An old man and an old woman who were tramps—tatterdemalions—and gentlefolks. I wondered who they were, and what their history was. I am stupidly and awkwardly shy at such times. My very wish to talk ties my tongue. It is difficult to talk without seeming curious, and curiosity would be an impertinence. The old people were well on in the years of age— nearly seventy, I should think. Their clothes were of the poorest, white at the seams, patched and mended in places with materials unlike the original stuffs, and frayed at the edges. But they were scrupulously clean.

Her hair was neatly plaited under the scarecrow bonnet. Their hands were white, and clean even to the nails. I never before saw clothes at once ragged and entirely clean. Queen-Mother-Ophelia was dirty and frowsy by their side. The old man was partly blind, and wore spectacles. He also wore a perpetual smile, sweet but feckless. The woman looked permanently scared, as if she had seen a ghost and never got over it. She stared with large grey eyes at everybody; but she managed her face (if I may so express it) well, and like a well-bred person. Her movements, when she arranged her ragged dress, folded her hands, or leant aside to talk to her companion, were well finished. She carried a small newspaper parcel. This, apparently, was their luggage. It consisted (as we found at last) of a very old packet of papers, yellow and torn, tied with string, and two thick slices of bread. One of these slices she gave to the old gentleman, the other she herself ate. There was no apology or confusion. It was all done with perfect manner. They were evidently very hungry.

I could not help watching them. I was afraid of seeming to show intrusive observations. I was able, however, to get a few words with the lady, and she spoke well. They chatted and laughed pleasantly together. He pointed out to her the features of the country near Tring, which he evidently knew thoroughly. He asked if a certain house was to be seen, . . . as . . . and here followed some story which interested them much. 'Ah!' he said at last, 'he's very rich now. I knew him well years ago. Poor man! Ah, well, he got a turn of fortune's wheel.' 'Well, dear,' I heard her say, 'your turn will turn next.' He laughed. 'Oh dear, no!' he said; 'that's not in my line. I turn the other way. It's luck; all luck—nothing else. I shan't get a turn now.' 'Never mind, dear,' said the woman; 'we're not unhappy, you know. And at least we're ourselves. And that is a great deal more than many people can say.'

When we neared London, he leant across to me and said, 'Can you tell me, sir, if the next station is Willesden? You see, I am rather blind, so I like to prepare myself for coming events.'

At Willesden they got out, walked arm-in-arm across the platform, and disappeared at the door of the station into the driving rain and mist. All they seemed to carry was the old paper packet done up in newspaper, and the abiding consciousness that they were themselves.

And that, after all, as the old lady said, is most emphatically a great deal more than many people can say.

Now, did any one ever meet such delightful people as these in a first-class carriage?

One has to own that 'first-class' people are apt to be more than a trifle dull. Then the best thing to do seems to be to look out of window. Sometimes I seem to have found good amusement there—as who cannot?—and occasionally the amusement found expression in my note-book, as the following passage about the fen country shows. I was travelling down from the North to London.

. . . The country near Peterborough was beautiful in the autumn sunshine. It is a country that has a very powerful appeal. The rushes and tall water-reeds that spring up here and there in the cornfields are full of suggestion. The thought goes back to the 'far-off unhappy times' when 'the brown horror of the homeless fen' was stretched out like a sea, and the Golden Borough on one side, and the stately fane of Ely on the other, rose like islands over the reed-ronds and 'tangled marish courses.' The dark purple soil has a voice and a story, and the flowers which blossom so luxuriantly in the dykes and long pools are pathetic in their beauty, as being the last traces of the old order that has yielded and given place to the new. One rejoices in the new order, and all it means; and one sees that it possesses a beauty too, a beauty of a higher type, though it exists in a lesser degree, than that of the old. But some minds, I suppose, turn naturally to the old order with a strange yearning. The picturesqueness and romance were perfected, and the beauty and romance of the new order are as yet only just begun. It is difficult to feel and discern the picture we are living in. Then, too, the idea of undisputed and untamed Nature has a fascination and wonder beyond words. It is this that, spite of legions of hotels and armies of tourists, still makes the snow of the Alps gleam with magic light. It is this that speaks to us so clearly and yet mysteriously in the wash of waves, and spreads the sands at low tide with miracle. And it is this which makes the thought of these fen-lands as they were before man's skill and patience and heroism had made them what they are, so beautiful a picture in the mind's eye. Nay, it is some faint trace of this, I think, which haunts the place even now. For Nature is still very strong here. The rein has to be held tight. She is gloriously indifferent everywhere, and will work man's will or her own with equal joy and fruition. But her will here is very antagonistic to his, and even in her obedience you read how great is the power compelled. Were the hand relaxed from the rein for but a moment, Nature would start away with riotous revolt. There are few parts of England where she is still so strong over so wide a tract of country.

To the painter and the poet these fen-lands are wonderfully beautiful, and it is conspicuous how both the pictures and verse of our generation record the fact. . . .

A sentence in the foregoing passage contains a word which is often on my lips, at least in thought—miracle. And in the note-book from which that passage is taken, I find, a few pages further on, another paragraph which suggests itself here as bearing on the thought contained in that word, so little used, and to my mind so often misused—miracle.

. . . I took a little walk before I started from

M—— this morning. Spring has come suddenly on us. It seemed to me that everything was awake and astir. There was a rustle of wings and a twitter of song; a smell of moist earth and of tender juicy buds, delicious to every sense. It scarcely seemed too fanciful to think that one heard a movement in the earth itself, and saw a pulse of awakening life.

Every year I live the lengthening days of spring, the shadows that lose their density and get purer in colour with the area of reflected light, as the light itself wins a longer daily arc, seem to be more glorious, adorable, miraculous. Spring and summer, autumn and winter, day and night, they all grow in wonder, beauty, and mystery. They are miracles, in truth, of eternal freshness. They reverse the experience we have of lesser things, and of matters the world delights to call miraculous. For these begin by seeming strange and wonderful, and by familiarity they lose their marvel more and more. But the simple root-facts of the world, as well as of our sojourn therein, gain new wonder, unspeakable, inexplicable, year by year. Miracles! Things, in the best and truest sense of the word, miraculous. As the old clergyman in *John Inglesant* says—' It seems to me, more and more, that the soul or spirit of every man passing through life among familiar things is among supernatural things always—always. And many things seem to me miraculous which men think nothing of.' I have often thought I should like to collect quotations from the great poets and thinkers about this miraculousness of daily life and of nature. They would form a wonderful and beautiful testimony. A voluminous one too. For I find most true poets and deep thinkers assert the fact that

> 'The common sun, the air, the skies,
> To them are opening Paradise.'

One gets wearied, in these days, of miracle-mongering and searchings after the occult, the mysterious, the marvellous, the veiled, and, let us add, the questionable. People find table-turning wonderful, and see no wonder in memory. They delight in I know not what mysteries of the far East, and see none in the rising sun. They would lift the veil from the unseen world, when the world around is already so veiled to them that they would do well to seek its revelations first. Such folks, however, would as a rule be the first to confess the authority of great poets and seers. They would emphasize the glory of the poet's mission. Let them listen, then, to what nearly all great poets say. For myself, I say with Walt Whitman—

> 'Why, who makes much of a miracle?
> As for me, I know nothing else but miracles.
> Every inch of space is a miracle;
> Every square yard of the surface of the earth is spread with the same.
>
> . . . .
> All . . . to me are unspeakable, perfect miracles. . . .'

The constant journeyings I had to take for my work gave me a large experience of change of residence—private houses and hotels. As a rule I always preferred to go to hotels. In fact, I soon found it necessary to make this rule, for many reasons. Hotels have been wonderfully improved in England during the last few years, and certainly, in the larger towns, comfort of a sufficient kind may be depended upon therein. I have, too, an ineradicable love for being my own master, and feeling 'at home.' The strangest hotel becomes home for the time; but there are many occasions when the *rôle* of guest—even of honoured and feasted guest—is fatiguing. Then most English houses in these days are temples of the wind.

'Fresh air' is a fashion, as universal neuralgia and rheumatism attest. And for myself, I am, in this matter, a born foreigner and alien. I love the open air, and would be in it—had I my will and a good climate—all day long, as foreigners often are. But, like them, I would have my rooms warm, and I call a draught anathema. So it is clear that I am a tiresome guest in an English country house. Nevertheless, my note-books are full of the records of pleasant visits—and of some amusing ones too. Occasionally I had a bad time of it, in breaking unknown ground. Once I remember —against my will and foreboding—being induced to accept an invitation to stay with people I knew not. I was to give a recital at an institute in the North, and I was told it was the rule for the members to take it in turn to entertain the lecturers, and that if I refused the invitation I should give dire offence. I therefore went. I chronicle the visit thus:

. . . What a terrible thing is Experience! How hollow, stale, flat, and unprofitable are her teachings! I picture her as a desolating, harsh-featured woman in drab, who does her best not only to spoil to-day, but also to embitter to-morrow by vague and prophetic croakings of dangers she will not describe and cannot prevent, and toward the practical softening of which—should they come—she will not put out a finger. Perhaps I am hard on this excellent and tiresome lady of the world unseen, but she has been hard on me, and I am smarting under the treatment.

I should say that it will teach me never again to lay myself open to a repetition of the annoyance. That is the sort of thing she likes to hear her victims say. Then she smiles grimly, for she knows there is no likelihood of a repetition. The next attack will come from another quarter, under another name, and wearing another guise. Her invention is great. She glories in defying detection. She lays wait and takes you by surprise. Therefore her teachings are for the most part simply gratuitous annoyances. They cannot be applied. Even the proverb owns that, tacitly—*Experientia docet.* Yes; but what it teaches, and how it is to be applied, is not stated. No; a disagreeable, disappointed woman!

Her last lesson to me has consisted of a visit to a small villa in an outlandish suburb of a big manufacturing town, entirely surrounded by brick-fields and the outlying works of a deserted foundry. The visit entailed a wayside station on a drizzling winter's afternoon; no 'flies' or cabs; no conveyances of any kind, save the hand-barrow of one deaf and partially paralyzed old man, who volunteered to bring up my luggage 'in the course of a couple of hours or thereabouts;' a long tramp through indescribably muddy lanes in the growing dusk; anon, small rooms, draughty as only small rooms know how to be; no fire in the bedroom; no hot water; no offer of tea; food that was desultory and unsafe; the key of the wine-cellar lost; no hope of a cab to the public hall; no possibility of one back; a hard pillow; and a child in the next room who was 'teething,' and protested all night long against the process.

That is the sort of thing Experience loves. And how can you apply the disagreeable lesson it teaches? The combination is very unlikely to occur again, at least in previously recognized form. Nevertheless, I have tried to wring some resolution for future guidance from it. I have hereon determined not to accept unknown invitations in my work, but always, always to go to a hotel. And what will be the result? I foresee it. I have refused an invitation for early next week for the recital at W——. I shall go to the hotel. Then I shall discover that the said hotel is abominable, and that I have refused to go to a charming house and delightful people.

Is not that the only sort of experience Experience ever gives? . . .

As far as I remember, my prognostications were entirely fulfilled. The hotel *was* abominable, and the invitation I had refused was to a house that I subsequently heard Mr. Oscar Wilde, who was giving lectures at the same set of institutes, say was altogether excellent and beautiful.

Of many of the pleasant and interesting visits I enjoyed it would not be fitting for me to speak in these pages, although my note-books have constant records of them. In houses, both great and small, I have found the most kindly welcome and hospitality, and have on more than one occasion gone to comparative strangers, and on departing felt that I was leaving friends. It was interesting, too, to see so many beautiful places; for surely no country in the world is so rich as ours in 'stately homes,' in fine estates, and in houses both pleasant and pretty, and often representing such a fulness and variety of daily living.

Once, when I had to go to Edinburgh for some work there, I had some very interesting visits in the neighbourhood. Through the kind introduction of Lady Caroline Charteris I went for a few days to Winton Castle, to stay with the late Lady Ruthven. She was a very remarkable woman. I was very glad to have that opportunity of knowing her, and I had many interesting talks with her. She was of a great age, and her memory was astonishing. Life, however, at that time was sorely and sadly narrowed to her, for she had lost her sight, and was very deaf. I never saw a braver struggle of a mind, still young, against failing bodily powers. But the gathering darkness was illuminated by the light of a faith that was to her the light of the world.

Like many deaf people, she had no idea of how to tone and modulate her voice; and this voice, being one of exceptional power, resounded through the rooms. Even when she fancied she was whispering, the matter in hand was published, as it were, from the housetop. One night, before dinner, she was settling how we were to go in. 'Let me see,' she said in the audiblest of stage whispers, 'there's Mr. Harrison. Who's he to take in? He's so shy! Let him have ——; she'll talk, and help him through.'

It recalled to my mind a memorable whisper I once heard in a drawing-room in London, at an afternoon party. It was at a great reading of a Shakespearean play. Royalty was listening. Many notabilities were present, both amongst audience and 'readers.' Amongst the former was Mrs. Grote. She sat in a corner with her friend Mrs. Duncan Stewart. The play had evolved itself well on into the fifth act. There was a pause before the last scene, and in the silence this whisper was heard from the corner where these two ladies sat: 'I'm so glad, my dear; they've turned over the last page. It'll soon be over now, and we shall have tea'!

In the country near Edinburgh there are a large number of beautiful and notable houses, and it was pleasant to see places whose names alone are like a bit of history. The sojourn in Edinburgh itself was interesting. The skies were kind and the air genial (it was midwinter) for a whole week, and Dunedin bewitched me with its beauty. Whilst there I had the pleasure of seeing (as I have already named) Dr. John Brown. Sir Noel and Lady Paton were most kind. His house and studio seems to hold the atmosphere of chivalry and romance which finds expression in his pictures. He has a very beautiful collection of armour, and many interesting relics of Mary Stuart. The first recital I gave in Edinburgh was at the house of the late Professor Sellar, and never have I had a more charming audience.

I stayed for some time with a very dear friend of mine, Mrs. Dunbar, at Preston Holme, near Newbattle. She was a very interesting woman, exceptionally clever, and with a rare faculty for the appreciation of art of all kinds. She was a granddaughter of Mr. Beckford, of Fonthill, and many were the interesting and extraordinary tales she could tell of her gifted and brilliant grandfather.* Surely never was the wail of the great king of old in Jerusalem more sardonically realized than it has been in the life of Beckford. Few people, outside a certain literary section, seem to know his name; and save on the title-page of his weird

* Mr. Beckford had two daughters—one became Duchess of Hamilton; the other married Colonel Orde, and was the mother of Mrs. Dunbar.

story of *Vathec*, it lives only in the ruined tower near Bath, as 'Beckford's Folly!'

What a hero he would make for a romantic novel! No element of romance seems wanting, even to the touch of mystery in his knowledge and love of things occult, and of the dark lore of the immemorial East. The tale of his life which Mrs. Dunbar told me was a veritable novel in itself, if only one might venture to write it down.

Mrs. Dunbar could tell ghost-stories better than any one I have ever met, save, perhaps, Mr. Augustus Hare. Her ghosts, perhaps, were not so accurate and exact as his, but I think they gained thereby in the attribute of mysticism. She often used to send me little invitations worded thus: 'Tea and ghosts, five o'clock.' I have sat in her boudoir at Preston Holme, in the dusk, by the firelight, and had a very excellent fit of 'the creeps' whilst she told, with graphic picturesqueness, some tale which would surely have been welcomed by the Psychical Society.

During this sojourn in Scotland I went to Hamilton, and whilst there Mrs. Dunbar took me over the Palace. That was before the great sale, and the place still held a Nibelungen hoard of treasure. I quote the page in my note-book which describes the visit. It was in the January of 1880.

. . . W—— and I went over the Palace this morning. Mrs. Dunbar acted as guide. No one could do it so well, for she knows every corner of it. The rooms in themselves, though numerous, do not seem to me individually as fine as those in some other great houses I have seen. But the name of the rooms is legion, and they are full of beautiful and costly things. The staircase of black marble is splendid.* The cabinets are numerous and of rare workmanship and materials. It was rather a shock to come across Botticelli's Last Judgment entirely surrounded and befrilled with pink and white calico in a *ruche*, part of some decorations put up for a ball.

We looked long at Romney's splendid picture of Beckford. He must have been a marvellously handsome man, both in face and form. The picture is in the library he collected. The rooms for the library were built by his daughter, the Duchess of Hamilton. There are some priceless old Missals in the collection. But we had not time, or strength, to see half the treasures.

* I believe it is now at Madame Tussaud's Exhibition.

After we had been through the Palace we went to the mausoleum in the park. It was built by the grandfather of the present duke for his own tomb, and it is certainly a most impressive resting-place. It possesses an echo that is phenomenal. 'Echo' seems scarcely the word to describe it. It is a symphony, a poem of the air. The air only needs a breath of sound, and it will evolve a drama. The mausoleum is a lofty circular tower with a domed roof. Inside, it is lit by a row of arched windows just under the dome. From the ground to these windows the walls rise in an unbroken surface to a great height. The light filters dimly down the well-like depth of the temple. The marbles and stones employed in the building are fine and choice, and the decoration is massive and appropriate. The brazen doors are richly wrought and of stately proportions. In the centre of the temple stands a sarcophagus, slightly raised. I believe the duke who lies within brought it from Egypt, and it was his wish that he himself should be buried in it. It was a curious form of pride to my mind, seeing that the tomb had clearly fulfilled its purpose once, and that therefore any second use must involve loss of dignity to the dumb occupant and to the receptacle. But pride is justified of all its children. To me the mummy-like shape of the thing, the strange devices carved on it —the serpent, the crocodile, the ibis, the bird-headed men, and the long procession of the departed spirits—should have kept the tomb sacred for ever. To appropriate it for one's self would seem to suggest alarming possibilities of the vengeance of unknown 'thrones, dominations, princedoms, powers.' But now, in spite of incongruity, it looks impressive enough—perhaps, indeed, a trifle over-impressive, verging on the uncanny and dreamlike, as it stands midmost this strange, dim temple of silence, dominating the place with symbols of altars that are cold. This symbolism, by the way, is the only one visible, as far as I recollect, of any altars at all.

We asked to be left alone in the place, and the servant left us, slamming the bronze gates. The silence leapt into thunderous life. Up and away to the dome the boom and clang reverberated in a deafening peal, resounding and re-echoing again and again, till it truly seemed 'to go right up to heaven, and die among the stars.' We permitted ourselves to give way to the strange influences of the place, and the incantation of its phantasmal voices. We spoke, and heard the invisible choirs of the air take up the words and make them their own, giving them beauty and derision, turning them to thunder and to sighs. We harmonized vocal chords, and the wall rang like an instrument—metallic, bell-like, flute-like, string-like—and in the end with the aerial softness of the zither. It was hard not to believe that there was a whole orchestra hidden away in that circular triforium under the domed roof. We realized the fact that the air has its waves and tides and ripples. We heard them. We heard the currents and streams of sound revolve, and meet and speak, as it were, on the air-waves; then rush apart again, and climb the walls like spray that is hurled against a rock. The air was void to the eye, but the ear recognized the fact that it was full, surcharged, heavy, and thick with impalpable substance of sound. One revolving detonation—when the doors were closed—lasted for nearly ten minutes. It died away, and remade itself, and changed from struggle to victory, and from victory into pain; and literally

'. . . Trembled away into silence
As if it were loth to cease.'

Adelaide Anne Procter's *Lost Chord* was realized here as the pretty conceit never could have been from the pipes of an organ and the vaulted aisles of a cathedral.

Somewhat abashed at the invisible audience, I spoke George Macdonald's fine verse—

'Alas! how easily things go wrong!
A sigh too much, or a kiss too long,
And there follows a mist and a weeping rain,
And life is never the same again.'

I made the last four words detach themselves from the others by tone and distinctness. Over the multitudinous echo-murmur and whisper of the other lines these few words rose and resounded through the building—'Never the same again! Never the same again!' Hundreds of voices seemed to say them, and each seemed to have some dismal idealization or caricature of the original utterance. A chorus of lost spirits could scarcely have been more eerie. Edgar Allen Poë might have given it expression.

We were almost glad to get out into the open air, and see the grey landscape lit toward the west with the pale fires of the winter sunset.

There is always something rather agitating in the presence of a power manifested and confessed, but wholly invisible. It seems the antithesis of the spectral, and is scarcely less disturbing.

END OF VOL. I.

www.ingramcontent.com/pod-product-compliance
Lightning Source LLC
Chambersburg PA
CBHW032054230426
43672CB00009B/1585